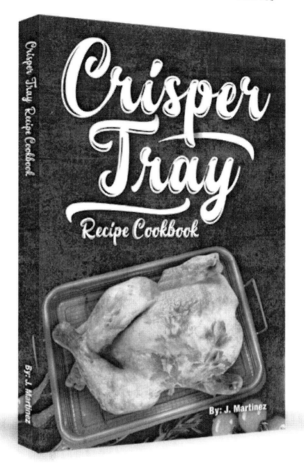

J. Martinez

HLR Press
Southern California

Crisper Tray Recipe Cookbook

LEGAL NOTICE

This information contained in this book is for entertainment purposes only. The content represents the opinion of the author and is based on the author's personal experience and observations. The author does not assume any liability whatsoever for the use of or inability to use any or all information contained in this book, and accepts no responsibility for any loss or damages of any kind that may be incurred by the reader as a result of actions arising from the use of the information in this book. Use this information at your own risk. No part of this book may be reproduced or transmitted in any form or by any means, electronic or mechanical, including photocopying, recording, or by any information storage or retrieval system, without express written permission from the author, except in the case of brief quotations embodied in critical articles and reviews – or except by a reviewer who may quote brief passages in a review.

The author reserves the right to make any changes he or she deems necessary to future versions of the publication to ensure its accuracy.

COPYRIGHT © 2017 / J. Martinez

All Rights Reserved.

Published In The United States of America By Healthy Lifestyle Recipes
www.Healthylifestylerecipes.org

By J. Martinez

FREE BOOKS!!

New Books, Pro Cooking Tips, & Recipes Sent to Your Email

For our current readers...if you like receiving free books, pro cooking tips & recipes to add to your collection, then **this is for you!** This is for promoting our material to our current members so you can **review our new books on Amazon** and give us feed back when we launch new books we are publishing! This helps us determine how we can make our books better for you, our audience! Just go to the url below and leave your name and email. We will send you a complimentary book about once a month.

[Get My Free Book]

http://www.Healthylifestylerecipes.org/Freebook2review

INTRODUCTION

This Crisper Tray Recipe Cookbook will keep you cooking like a pro in no time! This book will keep your delicious meals in check! You will notice when using your Crisper Tray that this is the only way you should be making meals your kitchen! This book will quickly give you the expertise you need to fully enjoy the benefits of non-stick cuisine. These recipes are very easy to read and right to the point! And that saves you time in the kitchen, which leaves more time for eating!

The Gluten Free section will also have you craving some of the special things that we have for you there. If you eat gluten free then you know that all of these recipes in this book can have substitutions for making foods that are right for you as well.

The select section in the back with all of the marinades you need to succeed! Juicy marinades for the meats of your choice will give your recipes that extra kick of flavor that you taste in all of your favorite restaurants..

Now...it's time to Enjoy the crispy deliciousness of these recipes...so get cooking!!

By J. Martinez

TABLE OF CONTENTS

Legal Notice	2
Free Books!!	3
New Books, Pro Cooking Tips, & Recipes Sent to Your Email	3
Introduction	4

CHAPTER 1:
Jump On The Band Wagon!! ... 7
Gotta Give It A Try! ... 7
Elite Recipes That Make You Look Like A Pro ... 7
Healthiest Way To Cook To Lower Cholesterol ... 7
"Toss Those Old Frying Pans..." ... 8
This Non-Stick Crisper Is All You'll Ever Need!

CHAPTER 2:
Make It Work For You! ... 9
Ultra-Durable And Scratch-Resistant ... 9
It's Like Frying...But No Grease! ... 9
100% Safe: PFOA, And PTFE-Free ... 9
Dishwasher Safe ... 10

CHAPTER 3:
Be A Master Crisper! ... 11
Don't Go Sticking Your Hand In A Fryer! ... 11
Step By Step; It's A Short Walk! ... 11
Too Much Time On Your Hands! ... 11
What's A Cook To Do? ... 11

CHAPTER 4:
Restaurant Quality At Home! ... 12
Grandma's Favorites! ... 12
Set the Table...Dinner's Almost Ready! ... 12
Bake or Grill, It's Up to You! ... 12
These Were Our Secret Recipes... Now They're Yours! ... 12

CHAPTER 5:
Perks & Benefits! ... 13
The Healthiest Choice In Cooking ... 13

CHAPTER 6
Ways to Clean Your Crisper? ... 14
Take Care Of What Takes Care Of You! ... 14
Super Material! ... 14
Clean As A New Pair of Sneakers! ... 14

CHAPTER 7
Cooking Tips To Becoming A "Pro" ... 15
Always Marinate Your Meats Before Cooking ... 15
Cooking With Meats That Have Fats ... 15
Know Your Fats & Oils: ... 16
"Cooking And Cholesterol"
Garnishing With Parsley: ... 16

CHAPTER 8
Foods Storage! ... 18
Store All Leftovers In Airtight, ... 18
Leak-Proof Containers
Separate Leftovers In Small ... 18
Containers To Cool Faster
Refrigerate Leftover Foods Within ... 19
Two Hours Of Cooking And Cooling
Divide Your Meats For A Longer & Safer Shelf Life ... 19
Food Temperature Safe Heating, Danger Chilling ... 20
and Freezing Zones!
Temperature Meat Baking Chart of Greatness! ... 21

BEEF: 23
Personal Mushroom Beef Wellington ... 23
Espresso Flavored Beef ... 25
Oven Roasted Barbeque Brisket ... 26
Orange Peel Marinated Pepper Steak ... 27
Sweet And Spicy Prime Rib ... 28
Oven Baked Chipotle Style Short Ribs ... 29
Oven Fried Garlic Smoked Cheeseburgers ... 30
Rolled All Beef Hot Dogs ... 31
Crisper Tray style Roast Beef ... 32
Argentinian Style Skirt Steak ... 33
Fiery Rolled Beef Tenderloin ... 34

CHICKEN: 35
Italian Style Rosemary Chicken Nachos ... 35
Tangy Roasted Basil Chicken Legs ... 37
Creamy Alfredo And Chicken Sausage Pizza ... 39
Cayenne Honey Herb Glazed Whole Chicken ... 40
Italian Style Cheesy Crusted Chicken ... 41
Chicken Tenders Sub Sandwich ... 43
Chicken and Pancakes ... 44
Chicken Rollatini ... 46
Oven Style Extra Crispy Fried Chicken ... 47
Hot & Tangy Chicken Wings ... 48
Boneless Chicken Tenders ... 49
Paprika Glazed Turkey Breast ... 50
Oven Fried Lemon Rotisserie Chicken ... 51
CRISPY But Juicy Baked Chicken Parm ... 52
Baked Lemon Thyme Chicken Wings ... 53
Baked Spicy Garlic Ranch Chicken Strips ... 54

LAMB: 55
Dijon Mustard Crusted Rack Of Lamb ... 55

PORK: 56
Ranch Style Pork Chops ... 56
Ham And Cheese Turnover ... 57
Sweet And Savory Bacon Wrapped Pork Tenderloin ... 58
Bacon Bread Garlic Rolls ... 59
Fried Cornflake Bacon ... 60
Toasted Coconut And Chocolate Baked Bacon ... 61
Sweet Cream Cheese Stuffed Jalapenos ... 62

Crisper Tray Recipe Cookbook

Bacon Wrapped Provolone Cheese Stuffed Dates 63
Bacon Stuffed Mushrooms 64
Ham Rolled Prawns... 65
Herb Crusted Pork Chops 66
Oven Fried Style Bacon... 68
Honey Dijon Pigs In A Blanket 69
With Tangy Mustard Sauce
Garlic Flavored Bacon Cheesey Fries 70
Baked Adobo Lime Steak Fajitas............................... 71

FISH: 72
Scallops With Brown Sugar Pear Sauce 72
Sautéed Halibut With Bacon Scallions...................... 73
Copper Crisper Style Salmon Cakes 74
Cheesy Baked Tuna Cakes.. 75
Oven Fried Fish Sandwiches 76
Cajun Style Catfish 78
Crab Cakes 79
Oven Fried Coconut Shrimp 80
Tex-Mex Cod Fish Cakes With Salsa 81
Baked Cajun "Square Pan Fried" Fish Strips 82

VEGETARIAN: 83
Vegetarian Sesame Seed Spring Rolls...................... 83
Vegetarian Style Ravioli 84
Eggplant Parmigiana Cakes.. 85
Melted Mozzarella Stuffed Onion Rings 86
Spicy Maple Syrup Twice Baked Sweet Potatoes.... 87
Parmesan Crusted Baked Zucchini 88
Oven Baked Herb Potatoes.. 89
Oven Fried Broccoli 90
Parmesan Roasted Corn On The Cob....................... 91
Garlic Sweet Potato Fries... 92
Roasted Onions And Peppers 93
Olive Oil Roasted Mushrooms 94
Asparagus Style Fries... 95
Rosemary Roasted Red Potatoes.............................. 96
Oven Roasted Vegetables 97
Crinkled Parsnips 98
Vegetable Pasta Salad.. 199
Cinnamon Sugar Sweet Potatoes........................... 101
Wedged Potato Chips 102

DESSERTS: 103
Golden S'more Cookies 103
Chocolate Chip Pan Cookies 104
Sheet Cake Fruit Cookies 105
Caramel Candy Pecan Pie Cookies......................... 106
Honey Plum Tarts 108
Fruity Infused Pizza.. 109
Cinnamon Style Donuts... 110
Oven Cinnamon French Toast Sticks...................... 111
Oven Fried Bananas... 112
Pastry Wrapped Milky Ways................................... 113

GLUTEN FREE: 114
For Those With Special Eating Needs 114
Gluten Free Monsterlicious Cookie Bars 115
Gluten Free Pork Pan Nachos 116
Gluten Free Oven Crispy Green Beans 117
Gluten Free Chicken and Vegetables 118
Gluten Free Sizzling Crispy Fried Fish 119
Gluten Free Savory Southern Fried Chicken 120
Gluten Free Oven Baked Buttermilk Doughnuts..... 121
Gluten Free Parmesan Style Pork Chops 123
Gluten Free Brown Sugar Oven Fried Steak 124
Gluten Free Garlic Cilantro Chicken....................... 125
Gluten Free Garlic Jalapeno Shrimp 126
Gluten-Free Bacon Stuffed Twice-Baked 127
Cheesy Garlic Potatoes
Gluten Free Spicy Crusted Asparagus 128
Gluten-Free Garlic Mint Mozzarella 129
Stuffed Meatballs
Gluten Free Crispy Lemon Dill Fish filet................. 130
Gluten Free Almond Crusted Garlic....................... 131
Basil Chicken Strips
Gluten Free Cinnamon Date Cranberry 133
Oatmeal Cookies

MARINADES: 134
Hand Selected For Meats & Veggies:..................... 134
Horseradish Apple Cider Garlic Marinade: 135
Garlic Rosemary Cinnamon Honey Marinade 136
White Wine Cayenne Pepper Kick Marinade........ 137
Red Wine Sweet Cajun Texas Tabasco Marinade... 138
Dill Lemon Pepper Basil Marinade 139
Louisiana Liquid Smoke Flavored Marinade 140
Pineapple Raspberry Flavor Twister Marinade...... 141
Garlic Italian Marinating Magnifier 142
Mild Marinade Seafood Soaker 143
White Wine Hot Peppered Garlic Marinade......... 144

Next On The List! 145
Here's What You Do Now.. 145

About The Author 146

Free Books!! 147
New Books, Pro Cooking Tips, & Recipes 148
Sent to Your Email

Other Recommend Books! 149

Recipe Notes 150

By J. Martinez

CHAPTER 1:
JUMP ON THE BAND WAGON!!

Gotta Give It A Try!

It's time to break away from the norm – away from the mess and frustration of trying to fry or bake and only receiving average results. This is why the Crisper Tray s great for your kitchen! The crisper is incredibly versatile and convenient, you're going to quickly forget about the time you almost burned down the house while frying on the stovetop. It's clean, safe, and fun, and in this book you will learn what it takes to master the Crisper Tray and look like a pro in front of your friends and family!

Elite Recipes That Make You Look Like A Pro

From beginners, to world-renowned chefs, our Crisper Tray and its accessory are super easy to use, clean and even store. For those who are new to the world of cooking, our Crisper Tray Utility Crisper Tray and this accessory should be your go to cookware of choice. You can make "easy cooking, healthy meals" in here that will have your friends and family cheering and in no time you can brush up on your cooking skills.

With the unique recipes that we have chosen from this playbook, you can become the type of cook that you want to be. (this product is so versatile that you can learn to oven bake (roast), stove top and grill your food just like any professional you've seen on tv and even one that would make your grandmother proud.)

Healthiest Way To Cook To Lower Cholesterol

The greatest thing about our Crisper Tray Utility Crisper Tray and its non stick cookie sheet accessory is that they are "super non-stick". Unlike most other kitchen ware, they do not require any fat or butter to keep food from sticking, flaking or breaking. Note: CRISPY FOOD that is NEVER FRIED! It's that simple! (a professional chef's trick of the trade!) Again, adding oils is not a must anymore but a choice…for flavor that is. This is important because all of that butter and fat could cause a person to have very high cholesterol. This Crisper Tray recipe cookbook is the healthier choice and helps lower your cholesterol one meal at a time.

"Toss Those Old Frying Pans..."
This Non-Stick Crisper Is All You'll Ever Need!

This is virtually the only non-stick utility that you will ever need to "Keep it Crispy!". The non-stick ceramic titanium coating is FREE from teflon, ptfe, and pfoa, thus allows your food to slide off of this basket and cookie sheet with ease, without the health risks that come with it. You can cook a variety of food on the product, even and do not have to worry about the sticky mess when you cook your meals. This tray and cookie sheet is so versatile that you can heat it up to very high temperatures and even throw that "bad boy" in the dishwasher for a safe clean. However, if you want to go old fashioned, you can clean it off with a rag and store it wherever you wish without worrying about the crisper getting scratched or ruined. Why wouldn't you want to add this great Crisper Tray to you or a loved one's cooking collection?

By J. Martinez

CHAPTER 2:
MAKE IT WORK FOR YOU!

Ultra-Durable And Scratch-Resistant

For this Crisper Tray we have done and found our own unofficial analysis to put this thing to the test but do not recommend you do this. You know...shopping for a Crisper Tray can be a pretty important task. After all, you are going to be cooking all of your food in this tray. So, you better make a good choice right? There are a variety of crispers to choose from. How do you choose the best one for you? Well, for starters, you want a Crisper Tray that will last a long time. I know that i would be furious if i bought a Crisper Tray and had to throw it away within a couple of months because of scratches and the fact that the coating was starting to peel off. How unhealthy and unsanitary is that?

Well, i will be the first to tell you that this ceramic titanium Crisper Tray is the best investment that you will ever make. Ceramic titanium is a lightweight metal coating and one of the strongest to be exact. The Crisper Tray has a type of coating that makes it scratch resistant, which means that you can use utensils on the base of the Crisper Tray and it will not scratch or peel the surface. The other great thing about this Crisper Tray is that it will never corrode or rust on you! "now that's a Crisper Tray you want in your kitchen!"

It's Like Frying...But No Grease!

You have all your ingredients ready, but you are out of oil or butter, or you are trying to lose weight, but you need to fry your food to make it crispy...What do you do? There is no need to worry because this Crisper Tray is super non-stick. This means that the food you cook with it doesn't need any oil or butter. You can cook everything you need without it. It's that simple! You will actually feel like you are cooking with grease because all of the food comes out crispy and slides right out and onto the plate.

100% Safe: PFOA, And PTFE-Free

We are all aware of the danger of Teflon style non-stick cookware. This is the brand that often gives non-stick kitchenware a bad reputation because they can cause many different types of health issues. First of all, Teflon is a type of coating that is owned by the Dupont Company. Teflon coating is often fluoropolymer plastic (PTFE), Perfluoroctanoic acid (PFOA) based. These chemicals are very harmful and can cause consumers to get very sick.

So, rest assured that this Crisper Tray is safe from all of that! This is one if the safest

Crisper Trays you can buy on the market by my opinion! This non-stick Crisper Tray does not contain these harmful chemicals! The lack of these chemicals make this product much safer for consumers and you can go about your cooking knowing that your health is safe!

Dishwasher Safe

After a long day of cooking, the last thing anyone wants to do is clean up the kitchen. Thank God for your dishwasher right? Wrong. Didn't you read that you couldn't put your non-stick kitchenware into the dishwasher and you had to refrain from certain soaps and other types of cleaners because they might ruin the surface of the Crisper Tray and cause it to erode? Well, you can scratch that with this one. Remember how this Crisper Tray is rust resistant, well,; it is dishwasher safe as well. Most non-stick Crisper Trays have a problem with dealing with high heats and this is the reason that you cannot put them in the dishwasher. This is not the case with the non-stick Crisper Tray. If you can put them in the oven, they would be able to survive the dishwasher, leaving you more time to do what you want and less time cleaning up the kitchen.

CHAPTER 3:
BE A MASTER CRISPER!

Don't Go Sticking Your Hand In A Fryer!

Before you show off, you might want to know what you're doing. More people today should take that approach, but that's another book on another topic. We aren't focusing on society here; we're focusing on your ability to know your way around a meal! The Crisper Tray is designed to help you look good and keep your kitchen clean: it's that simple. So what do I have to do? Spoiler alert: not much.

Step By Step; It's A Short Walk!

Simply prep your dish and preheat the oven. Got it? Okay, we're moving along already. Let's go out on a limb and say you prepared some delicious fried chicken. If not, pretend you did. Place your tenders and drumsticks in the Copper Crisper, put the tray on the baking sheet, and slide into the oven. Got it? Man, we're good at this. Cook at your desired time and temperature and that's all she wrote!

Too Much Time On Your Hands!

Cookie sheets, deep solid pans, and aluminum get little ventilation, forcing you to monitor and turn your food occasionally. With the Copper Crisper's elevated mesh design, you're off the hook! No checking, no turning. And unlike other mesh trays, the baking sheet below catches the crumbs and drips. So now you can use those extra minutes for something more productive like cleaning up. Wait, you don't have to do that either. There will be no grease splattered all over the stove and counters, and there will be no fat to jar afterwards. Whatever will you do with your time?

What's A Cook To Do?

So you have no grease, you have no fat, and you have no mess. I suggest it's time to get a little creative with your recipes then! Considering the Crisper Tray is so convenient and versatile, you can spend your time coming up with new creations and preparing mouthwatering meals!

CHAPTER 4: RESTAURANT QUALITY AT HOME!

Grandma's Favorites!

All those deep-fried standards like chicken tenders, French fries, mozzarella sticks, stuffed mushrooms, and jalapeno poppers can all be created in the convenience of your own home with the Crisper Tray. Impress with onion rings, show off your skills with pigs in a blanket, and appease the health nuts with fresh roasted vegetables! All your favorites can be made in your oven or on your grill with ease!

Set the Table...Dinner's Almost Ready!

The final product is what keeps people coming back, and even classic standards stand out. However, the Crisper Tray opens up a world of new ideas. **For example:** you don't have to wait for a trip to Maryland to have fresh crab cakes, you don't need to reserve a table at a fancy Italian restaurant to enjoy creamy and crispy Chicken Florentine, and you don't have to run to the bakery for dessert when you can get creative with sweet little Valentine's Day pizzas! The possibilities are endless; it's just up to you to create!

Bake or Grill, It's Up to You!

We've been talking about the convenience and uniqueness of the Crisper basket, but your cooking doesn't need to change with this product; in fact, it makes it healthier and easier! You can still bake and grill, but the design doesn't trap the grease and fat which provides even more room for your flavors to shine.

These Were Our Secret Recipes... Now They're Yours!

Your secret marinade? Still good to smother your food in. Your secret spicy rub? Still okay to cover your dish in. That recipe you stole from the pros? Even better on the Copper Crisper. Your great grandmother's recipe no one will ever see? Your ancestors should have tasted what you made! The Crisper Tray allows you to be you, but with more convenience.

CHAPTER 5: PERKS & BENEFITS!

The Healthiest Choice In Cooking

We live in an age where people are starting to be more health conscious. We see this in everything that we do, from ads on tv to what we read in magazines. Why would our cookware be any different? This is where we cook the food that goes into our bodies. So, of course this is going to be important to us. Most of the food that we cook requires oils and butter so that food does not stick to the cookware.

Well, we no longer need to worry about that. This non-stick Crisper Tray requires no oils or butters. The non-stick coating that is on the base of the Crisper Tray keeps foods from sticking. That's the whole purpose of the Crisper Tray, but it is a major health benefit to us. Of course we need some oils or fat to help our skin, this is where a little bit of olive, avocado or coconut oil can be used for some flavor, or just to brush over the food to make it extra crispy. Just remember that this is not an essential ingredient for cooking anymore, rather a choice. But these oils that we just mentioned are really good for you and can benefit your body as well as your cooking.

CHAPTER 6
WAYS TO CLEAN YOUR CRISPER?

Take Care Of What Takes Care Of You!

The Crisper Tray keeps your oven or grill clean, so now it's time to do the same for this delightful product. Return the favor! Not surprisingly, this doesn't take a whole lot of effort to accomplish.

Super Material!

The Crisper Tray is made of stainless steel and the baking sheet is made of aluminum. Both are coated with non-stick copper coloring so there will be no more pesky glops of burned food and grease to scrape off afterward. The coat will not peel or chip, and there is no need for polish!

Clean As A New Pair of Sneakers!

There are two easy ways to clean this Crisper. The most recommended form is to hand wash in water with mild soap or cleanser. If you want to save even a little more time, you're in luck, because the Crisper Tray is also dishwasher save. Remember, before your first use, don't forget to give it a light wash with non-abrasive soap. Cleaning up is as easy as getting started!

By J. Martinez

CHAPTER 7
COOKING TIPS TO BECOMING A "PRO"

Always Marinate Your Meats Before Cooking

You often think of marinating your steak or chicken breast during barbeque season. What if i told you that marinating your meat was actually good for your health? Well, it is. Marinating your beef, poultry and fish can help decrease the carcinogenic heterocyclic amines (hcas) that are produced when meat is grilled or cooked at high temperature levels. Marinating the meat first can reduced these levels by 99 percent, and if you add a touch of rosemary to the marinade that you make, it could help decrease this even more.

There are a few more reasons why using marinates can be beneficial to your meats prior to cooking. For instance, the acidic quality within the marinade can help slow down bacteria growth (when using citrus juices and vinegars.) But remember to always keep your meats soaking with your marinated in the fridge where your meats will stay cool and safe. Another great thing about marinates, besides the flavor, is that the juices can also tenderize the meat for you. This will help with digestion, so that the meat goes down smoothly. Lastly, marinates help keep the meat moist. So, you will never have to hear your mother-in-law tell you that your meat is dry and tough. ...and that's one to grow on!

Cooking With Meats That Have Fats...

Is This A Substitute For Oil And Butter? Well...this is really a topic to talk about! If you are cooking with oils and butter, and also have fats on the meat that you are cooking with...you are just adding more oils to the cooking process. This will increase the fat content of your foods tremendously, and this is what you will be eating as a result of that! If there are recipes that call for oils or butter...check to see how much fat is on the meat. I know that you cannot calculate this precisely, but if you are aware that the meat you are cooking with has fat on it then you can scale back the amount of oil (or butter) that you are cooking with. This only makes sense because the recipe does not know how much fat is on your meat anyway. The fat content on meats will not only be a fat substitute, but it will also be something that flavors your foods in the process! If you cut down the amount of oil, grease and butter that you are cooking with you will be eating and serving much healthier recipes, keeping your cholesterol levels lower from not using that additional oil in your foods. Now…that's one to grow on! :)

Know Your Fats & Oils: "Cooking And Cholesterol"

There is something to say about vegetable oils. They are the most "all-purpose oils" and probably the least expensive types of oils to cook with. There are oils that you may not have noticed or considered as an alternative to cook with, and here are just a few to keep in mind. Almond oil, coconut oil, grape seed oil and avocado oils, just to name a few for a little range of variation and diversity.

There are other oils that are great for foods but you may think about the heat exposure because these oils burn very easily when exposed to high cooking temperatures. These oils are normally utilized best when added to a salad or even a nice pasta dish or even best on vegetables for that added flavor! Such oils consist of oils that come from different types of nuts, sesame oil and we don't want to forget that extra virgin olive oil!

One oil that is extremely popular and not as expensive as the ones that were just mentioned is an "all favorite" the regular olive oil! This type of oil is a great cooking oil and adds a good flavor to your foods as well but just keep in mind again about the temperature that you are cooking with because this is one that can burn at high temperatures as well! Just read the labels to see which different flavors will go best with the foods you are cooking, and keep in mind the amount of heat that the oils can withstand…" and that's another one to grow on!"

Garnishing With Parsley:

It's More Than Just For Decoration!
We are all familiar with the green leafed tree that decorates our plates at restaurants. Did you know that parsley was actually more than a garnish? This herb is a jack of all trades in the culinary world, and should be treated as such. First of all, the herb is packed with vitamin a, b, c, e, k, and it's great for your digestion. No wonder chefs have been putting it on your plate for years. It is supposed to be eaten after your meal. However, parsley can be used to eliminate waste, maintain gas, and relieves bloating, water retention and does this with its anti-inflammatory substances. This little green garnish can even help freshens your breath. So, grab a leaf and bon a petite.

By J. Martinez

Parsley should be called the next Superfood. Not only is it packet with a ton of vitamins, but it can be used as an antibiotic and may aid against other bodily illnesses or infections as well. As an antibiotic, parsley boosts the immune system and may also help prevent other things like the common cold or flu, as well as treat bladder and urinary tract infections. The herb also contains high amounts of apigenin, which is an anticancer property. Eating parsley may help reduce the risk of beast, skin, prostrate and other cancers. The herb can also be used as an anti-inflammatory, as well as a detoxifier; eating it will definitely help keep you healthy. So, the next time a chef adorns your plate with a leaf of parsley, you should thank her for caring about your health enough to put it on your plate.

CHAPTER 8
FOODS STORAGE!

Have you ever cleaned out your fridge and noticed all of the food that was sitting in your garbage can? Throwing food away can be very expensive and believe me, no one likes throwing money into the trash. This is one of the reasons why knowing the right ways to preserving your food is so important. This chapter will provide tips on how to store your food to avoid foodborne illnesses, preserve its shelf life and even save money.

Store All Leftovers In Airtight, Leak-Proof Containers

Food safety is important when it comes to protecting our health. One of the best ways to do this is to store all of your leftovers from tonight's meal in air-tight, leak-proof containers. These containers protect against air-borne bacteria, pests and even leaks. When used correctly, they will protect the shelf life, taste and longevity of your leftovers. Now you and your family can continue to enjoy them for a little bit longer.

Glass containers with snap on lids are the best containers to use when storing food. Plastic containers can stain when storing food, such as spaghetti sauce or enchiladas. Glass containers do not stain as easily. Also, when storing food in plastic containers it is hard to see what is actually inside them. Storing food in glass containers help you see what is inside. Remember to label the date that you cooked and stored the food. This will give you a good idea of how old it is and when you need to dispose of it.

Separate Leftovers In Small Containers To Cool Faster

There is a myth about storing hot or warm food in the fridge right away. Many people say that when you place large amounts of hot food into the fridge before cooling it down, it can cause the temperature to rise in the fridge, which can warm up all of the other food inside as well. So, the hot food will not only cool down rapidly, but it will warm up everything else. Even if this is the case, refrigerators were invented to keep food cool and not be affected by the warmth of newly

By J. Martinez

cooked food. It is far more dangerous to let food sit out at room temperature to cool then to place it in the fridge while it is still warm.

When cooking large amounts of food, like stews, it can be easier to separate the leftovers into small containers. This can be beneficial for two reasons. First, it will allow the food to cool down much faster and at a safer temperature. Putting the food in more than one container lets it cool down without the risk of spoiling outside of the container or making the other food in the fridge warmer. Secondly, it becomes convenient for reheating small amounts for lunch or an individual dinner at home. Reheating the food in the microwave more than once can cause problems as well. So, this eliminates the problem of warming up more than you can eat at one time.

Refrigerate Leftover Foods Within Two Hours Of Cooking And Cooling

Refrigerating or freezing leftovers to preserve them is important. It is not only a healthy tip, but a financial one as well. In order to make sure that we and our families are eating healthy food, we need to make sure that we are preserving it correctly. Bacteria grows at a fast rate between the 40º f and 140º f range. Hot food must be kept at 140º f or higher to prevent bacteria. Food must be refrigerated at 41º f or lower to prevent everyone from getting sick.

Store your leftovers within two hours of cooking food and within one hour, if the temperature in the room is over 90 degrees. It is very important to adhere to these safety tips because it can be harmful to your health or that of your family if you don't. These tips can help keep you from getting sick from the bacteria that lingers around improperly handled food.

Divide Your Meats For A Longer & Safer Shelf Life

Just like fruits and vegetables, separating leftover meat is important to maintaining a longer shelf life. Cooling the meat and putting them in shallow or separate containers keeps it fresh longer. Divide the large portions into smaller quantities. If the food cooked in a very hot container then you want to put it into a container that doesn't keep it from cooling. One thing also to remember is not to pack the food tightly in the container or the refrigerator. Keeping a proper airflow helps maintain the temperature in the meat and helps it cool off. This way it will last longer and will be easy to grab when you want a good snack. All you have to do now is enjoy now and later!

Food Temperature Safe Heating, Danger Chilling and Freezing Zones!

A guide for food temperature cooking!

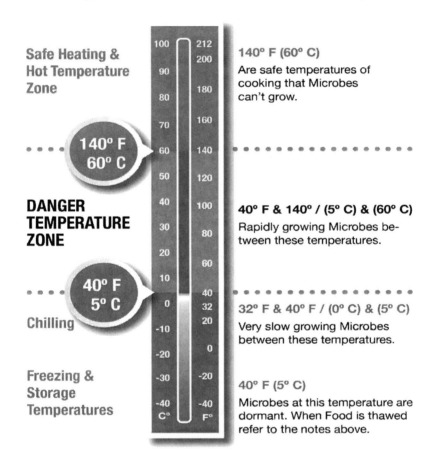

Safe Heating & Hot Temperature Zone

140° F (60° C)
Are safe temperatures of cooking that Microbes can't grow.

DANGER TEMPERATURE ZONE

40° F & 140° / (5° C) & (60° C)
Rapidly growing Microbes between these temperatures.

Chilling

32° F & 40° F / (0° C) & (5° C)
Very slow growing Microbes between these temperatures.

Freezing & Storage Temperatures

40° F (5° C)
Microbes at this temperature are dormant. When Food is thawed refer to the notes above.

By Elana Cordova

Temperature Meat Baking Chart of Greatness!

Baking	Temperature	Cooking Time
BEEF		
Sirloin or Rib Roast	325 degrees	20-25 minutes
Rump, Round (Roast)	275 degrees	45-50 minutes
VEAL		
Leg, Loin, Rib Roast	325 degrees	35-40 minutes
PORK		
Leg or Loin	325 degrees	20-25 minutes
Crown Roast	325 degrees	15-20 minutes
Shoulder Roast	325 degrees	25-30 minutes
HAM		
Smoked, Pre-Cooked	325 degrees	10-15 minutes
LAMB		
Leg	350-400 degrees	20-25 minutes
Leg, Shoulder Roast	325 degrees	25-30 minutes
Rack (Roast)	400 degrees	20-25 minutes
POULTRY		
Turkey	325 degrees	4-5 hrs / 10-14lbs
Chicken	375 degrees	2.5-3.5hrs / 4-6lbs
Duckling	325-350 degrees	2-3 hrs / 4-5 lbs
Capon	325-350 degrees	2.5-3.5hrs /6-8lbs
Goose	325 degrees	4-5 hrs / 10-12lbs

Crisper Tray Recipe Cookbook

Reason for the frying chart. – We understand that everything you cook won't go in the crisper so we added this temperature chart for you to use with your other cooking needs.

Frying	Temperature	Cooking Time
Bacon	300-325 degrees	8-10 minutes
Canadian bacon	275-300 degrees	3-4 minutes
Chicken	325-350 degrees	25-40 minutes
Eggs, fried	250-275 degrees	3-5 minutes
Eggs, scrambled	250-275 degrees	3-5 minutes
Fish	325-375 degrees	5-10 minutes
French Toast	300-325 degrees	4-6 minutes
Ham ½ thick	325-350 degrees	10-12 minutes
Ham ¾ thick	325-350 degrees	14-16 minutes
Hamburgers	325-375 degrees	8-12 minutes
Minute Steak	375-400 degrees	4-5 minutes
Pork Chops ½ thick	325-375 degrees	15-20 minutes
Pork Chops ¾ thick	325-375 degrees	20-25 minutes
Potatoes	300-350 degrees	10-12 minutes
Sausage, link	300-325 degrees	20-30 minutes
Sausage, precooked	325-350 degrees	10-12 minutes
Sandwiches, grilled	300-325 degrees	5-10 minutes
Steak, rare	350-400 degrees	6-7 minutes
Steak, medium	350-400 degrees	10-12 minutes

By J. Martinez

BEEF:

Personal Mushroom Beef Wellington

This elegant dish is something you would order in high class restaurant, but now you can make it in your very own kitchen, and in under an hour nonetheless.

Total Time: 40 minutes
Makes: 6 Servings

INGREDIENTS:
- 1 lb. cremini mushrooms
- ¼ cup Italian dressing
- 1 small shallot, finely chopped
- ½ cup Parmesan Cheese, grated
- 1 tbsp. parsley, finely chopped
- 6 beef tenderloin steaks, 1 inch thick
- 2 tsp. ground peppercorns
- 1 tbsp. oil
- 1 frozen puff pastry sheet, thawed
- 1 egg, beaten

DIRECTIONS:
- Set the oven to 450 degrees.
- Start by adding the mushrooms to a food processor. Make sure they are finely chopped.
- Using a small skillet, heat the Italian dressing.
- Now, add the mushrooms and cook for 2 minutes.
- Add the shallots and cook for another 2 minutes.
- Transfer the mushrooms and shallots into a bowl and add the cheese and parsley.
- Next, season the steaks with the peppercorns. Make sure to season evenly.
- Place the steaks in the Copper Crisper Tray .
- Cook for 15 minutes.
- Let cool.
- To prepare the pastry: Flour a cutting board

- Unfold the pastry. Make sure to roll on 20x12 inch rectangles.
- Cut into 6 squares.
- Spoon the mixture into the center of each square, and then top with the steak.
- Close the edges of the pastry together and pinch.
- Place the pastry upside down on the Copper Crisper cookie sheet.
- Cut slits in each pastry for air and brush with the egg.
- Cook for 14 minutes.
- Let the beef wellington stand for 10 minutes. Serve and enjoy.

By J. Martinez

Espresso Flavored Beef

The strong flavor of espresso gives this beef a new and inspiring flavor. One that will knock your socks off and make you wonder why you never thought of paring these two together before.

Total Time: 70 minutes
Makes: 4 Servings

INGREDIENTS:
- 1 4 lb. beef tenderloin
- 2 tbsp. ground espresso
- 2 tbsp. coffee
- 1 tbsp. brown sugar
- 1 ½ tsp. ground coriander
- 1 ¼ tsp. paprika
- ¾ tsp. sea salt
- ½ tsp. black pepper
- ¼ tsp. cayenne
- ½ tsp. garlic powder
- Olive oil

- Directions:
- Set the oven to 425 degrees.
- Start with mixing the brown sugar, coffee, espresso, and the rest of the spices together.
- Season the beef with the rub. Make sure to coat evenly.
- Brush the olive oil all over the meat.
- Place on the Copper Crisper Tray .
- Cook for 60 minutes.
- Let rest for 15 minutes.
- Slice the meat into strips then serve and enjoy.

Oven Roasted Barbeque Brisket

Brisket is one of those dishes that remind us of grandma's cooking. This version will have your grandma asking you to cook for the next holiday.

Total Time: 145 minutes
Makes: 16 Servings

INGREDIENTS:
- 1 4 lb. beef tenderloin
- 1 red onion, thinly sliced into rings
- 1 cup barbeque sauce
- 1 lb. red potatoes cut into chunks
- 1 lb. yellow potatoes cut into chunks
- 1 lb. carrots, sliced

DIRECTIONS:
- Set the oven to 325 degrees.
- Place the brisket in the Copper Crisper cookie tray.
- Pour the onions and barbeque sauce on top.
- Cook for 2 hours.
- Take out and place the potatoes and carrots around the meat.
- Cook for another hour.
- Set the potatoes, and vegetables aside.
- Cut the meat into strips.
- Serve with vegetables and sauce from the sheet.

By Elana Cordova

Orange Peel Marinated Pepper Steak

Citrus is one of the best ingredients to pair with meat. It doesn't disappoint in this dish either.

Total Time: 81 minutes
Makes: 8 Servings

INGREDIENTS:
- ½ cup Catalina dressing
- 1 medium orange, grated peel and juice
- 1 medium lemon, zest and juice
- 2 green onions, chopped
- ½ tsp. pepper
- ½ tsp. garlic salt
- 1 2lb. boneless beef sirloin steak

DIRECTIONS:
- Set the oven to 350 degrees.
- Start with mixing the salad dressing, lemon juice, lemon peel, orange peel, orange juice, onions, pepper, and garlic together.
- Remove ¼ of the mixture for later use.
- Place the meat in the mixture and coat evenly,
- Marinate for 1 hour.
- Take out the steak and place it in the Copper Crisper Tray .
- Cook for 15 minutes, turning it over halfway through.
- Let the steak rest and then slice into 8 pieces.
- Drizzle the rest of the salad dressing mixture on top.
- Serve and enjoy.

Sweet And Spicy Prime Rib

Sweet and spicy prime rib? Yes. We are taking a classic away from the drum of horseradish and adding yellow mustard with honey and brown sugar. This way you get a little heat with your sugar.

Total Time: 70 minutes
Makes: 15 Servings

INGREDIENTS:
- 1 beef prime rib roast
- ½ tsp. coarse black pepper, divided
- ¼ tsp salt
- 2 tbsp. butter
- 2 cups mixed mushrooms, sliced
- 2 tbsp. flour
- 2 tbsp. yellow mustard
- 2 tbsp. brown sugar
- 1 tsp. honey
- ¼ tsp. dried thyme leaves
- ¼ tsp. ground sage
- ¼ ground parsley
- 1 ½ cups beef broth
- ¼ cup Marsala wine

DIRECTIONS:
- Set the oven to 325 degrees.
- Place the meat in the Copper Crisper Tray .
- Season with salt and pepper.
- Cook for 2 ½ hours.
- Rest for 10 minutes.
- Next, in a saucepan, melt butter.
- Add mushrooms and cook for 3 minutes.
- Now, stir in flour, mustard, brown sugar, honey, herbs and the rest of the pepper together.
- Lastly, add the broth and wine.
- Cook for 4 minutes and Serve the meat with the sauce.

By Elana Cordova

Oven Baked Chipotle Style Short Ribs

Chipotle style short ribs are a great BBQ dish that you can make year round and the adobo marinated chipotle peppers adds a flavor that is not usually paired with ribs.

Total Time: 60 minutes
Makes: 6 Servings

INGREDIENTS:
- *1 can beef broth*
- *½ cup barbeque sauce*
- *3 canned chipotle peppers in adobo sauce*
- *2 ¼ tsp. honey*
- *2 tbsp. flour*
- *2 lb. beef short ribs*
- *1 ¼ tbsp. fresh cilantro, chopped*
- *3 cups rice, cooked*

DIRECTIONS:
- Set the oven to 350 degrees.
- Mix the beef broth, barbeque sauce, chipotle peppers, and honey together in a blender.
- Blend until smooth.
- Next, pour the flour in a bowl.
- Dip the ribs into the flour on both sides.
- Place the ribs in the Copper Crisper Tray and cook in batches.
- Cook for 5 minutes.
- Remove from the basket and place the ribs on the Copper Crisper cookie tray.
- Pour the sauce on top of the ribs.
- Cook for another 1 ½ hours.
- Sprinkle the cilantro on top and serve with the rice.

Oven Fried Garlic Smoked Cheeseburgers

Who thought you could make cheeseburgers in the oven? With the Crisper Tray … now you can.

Total Time: 12 minutes
Makes: 4 Servings

INGREDIENTS:
- 1 lb. Lean ground beef
- 1 tbsp. Worcestershire sauce
- 1 tsp. Maggi seasoning sauce
- Few drops liquid smoke
- ½ tsp. garlic powder
- ½ tsp. onion powder
- Four slices of cheddar Cheese

DIRECTIONS:
- Set the oven temperature at 350 degrees.
- Start with mixing the seasonings in a small bowl.
- In a medium bowl, combine the hamburger and spices.
- Separate the mixture into four parts and form into a ball.
- Place the burgers in the Crisper Tray and bake for 10 minutes.
- Place cheese on top of each hamburger and let bake for an additional 2 minutes until melted.
- Serve on lettuce, or buns and enjoy.

By Elana Cordova

Rolled All Beef Hot Dogs

A familiar appetizer cooked more thoroughly. Who doesn't love rolled hot dogs?

Total Time: 10 minutes
Makes: 4 Servings

INGREDIENTS:
- *Package of 8 All Beef Hot Dog Wieners*
- *Package of 8 Pop Open Crescent Rolls*

DIRECTIONS:
- Set the oven temperature at 375 degrees.
- Start with separating the crescent rolls into 8 triangles.
- Roll each triangle around each individual hot dog and drop them into the Crisper Tray leaving space between each one.
- Bake for 10 minutes, serve with dipping sauce and enjoy.

Crisper Tray style Roast Beef

Want to make an easy familiar dinner on a busy night? Have no fear. This recipe is fast, easy and delivers a succulent piece of meat.

Total Time: 25 minutes
Makes: 4 Servings

INGREDIENTS:
- 2 lb. chuck roast
- Kosher or sea salt to taste
- Freshly ground pepper to taste

DIRECTIONS:
- Set the oven temperature at 450 degrees.
- Start with pouring oil over the roast and seasoning it.
- Place the roast in the Crisper Tray , fat side up.
- Bake for 15 minutes.
- Let the roast cook until it reaches 124 degrees for rare, 145 for medium, and 160 for well done.
- Let the roast rest for 10 minutes and serve when done.

By J. Martinez

Argentinian Style Skirt Steak

The sauce will bring you to a South American paradise.

Total Time: 30 minutes
Makes: 4 Servings

INGREDIENTS:
- 16 oz. skirt steak
- 1 cup parsley, washed and finely chopped
- ¼ cup mint, washed and finely chopped
- 2 tbsp. oregano, washed and finely chopped
- 3 cloves garlic, finely chopped
- 1 tsp. crushed red pepper
- 1 tbsp. ground cumin
- 1 tsp. cayenne pepper
- 2 tsp. smoked paprika
- 1 tsp. salt
- ¼ tsp. black pepper
- 3 tbsp. Red wine vinegar

DIRECTIONS:
- Set the oven temperature at 350 degrees.
- Start with mixing all of the ingredients together.
- Cut the steak in portions.
- Place the steak and ¼ of the sauce in a re-sealable bag.
- Marinate in the fridge for 2 hours.
- Remove the steak and let rest for 30 minutes.
- Place the chicken in the Crisper Tray and cook for 8 minutes.
- Garnish with the sauce, serve and enjoy.

Fiery Rolled Beef Tenderloin

Creating an onion and herb mixture for this recipe gives a twist to beef tenderloin.

Total Time: 40 minutes
Makes: 4 Servings

INGREDIENTS:
- *1 lb. beef tenderloin*
- *1 clove garlic, crushed*
- *½ tsp. chili powder*
- *1 tsp. cinnamon*
- *1 ½ tsp. ground cumin*

DIRECTIONS:
- Start with placing the meat tenderloin on a cutting board and slice it horizontally.
- Mix the garlic, chili powder, cinnamon, cumin, pepper, salt, and olive oil together.
- Spoon a tbsp. of the mixture in a small bowl and add the onion and parsley into the mixture.
- Set the oven temperature to 375 degrees.
- Rub the onion mixture on the outside of the meat and roll securely with string.
- Next, rub the mixture on the outside of the meat.
- Place the tenderloin in the Crisper Tray and bake for 40 minutes.
- Rest for 10 minutes and slice.
- Serve and enjoy.

By Elana Cordova

CHICKEN:

Italian Style Rosemary Chicken Nachos

Nachos made Italian style. Who doesn't love garlic flies topped with cheese and meat? The flavors of this dish will wow you.

Total Time: 30 minutes
Makes: 4 Servings

INGREDIENTS:
- 2 boneless, skinless chicken breasts
- 1 24 oz. package of rosemary garlic oven fries
- 1 zucchini, sliced
- 1 yellow squash, sliced
- 3 slices bacon, chopped
- 1 tsp. Italian seasoning
- 1 tsp. parsley
- 1 tsp. basil
- 2 tbsp. olive oil
- 1 ½ cup Italian five-cheese blend, shredded
- 1 pint grape tomatoes, halved
- 1 garlic clove, chopped
- 2 tsp. balsamic vinegar
- 1/3 cup fresh basil leaves, torn
- ½ red onion, for garnish

DIRECTIONS:
- Set the oven to 475 degrees.
- Place the garlic fries, bacon and, yellow squash, zucchini on the Copper Crisper cookie sheet.
- Cook for 15 minutes.
- Next, sprinkle the chicken with the salt, pepper, basil, parsley, and Italian seasoning
- Set aside the garlic fries
- Place the chicken on the baking sheet and cook for 30 minutes.

- Chop the chicken into pieces.
- Pour the potatoes in the middle of the cookie sheet and top with the cheeses and the chicken.
- Cook for 4 minutes.
- While cooking, mix the tomatoes, garlic, olive oil, salt, pepper and balsamic vinegar together.
- Spoon on top of the nachos and serve.

By J. Martinez

Tangy Roasted Basil Chicken Legs

Oven baked chicken can get pretty drab. However, not with this recipe! The tanginess of this chicken, combined with herbs, broccoli and potatoes will add a little color to this common family dish.

Total Time: 30 minutes
Makes: 4 Servings

INGREDIENTS:
- *8 medium drumsticks*
- *1 24 oz. package frozen steam and mash cut potatoes*
- *¼ cup all-purpose flour*
- *1 tbsp. all-purpose flour*
- *3.4 cup chicken stock*
- *¼ cup white wine*
- *½ heavy cream*
- *2 cups Dijon mustard*
- *2 tsp. fresh thyme, chopped*
- *2 tsp. fresh basil, chopped*
- *2 tsp. fresh parsley, chopped*
- *2 bunches broccoli*
- *1 tbsp. olive oil*
- *1 lemon, sliced*
- *2 garlic cloves, chopped*
- *Salt to taste*
- *Pepper to taste*

DIRECTIONS:
- Set the oven to 350 degrees.
- Start with preparing the potatoes according to the directions.
- Sprinkle salt and pepper on the drumsticks.
- Next, mix the chicken with the flour.
- Place the drumsticks in the Copper Crisper Tray .
- Cook for 30 minutes.
- Now, mix together the heavy cream, chicken stock, white wine, Dijon mustard, flour, thyme, basil and parsley together.

- Pour on top of the chicken halfway through
- When done cooking, place the broccoli, lemon, garlic and olive oil on the Copper Crisper cookie tray.
- Cook for 8 minutes.
- Serve chicken on top of the potatoes with the broccoli and enjoy.

By J. Martinez

Creamy Alfredo And Chicken Sausage Pizza

The kids love homemade pizza night, but what about pizza for the grownups? Forget pepperoni and add chicken sausage. Forget marinara sauce and add creamy Alfredo, and paired with a nice glass of wine. We promise that you will not be disappointed.

Total Time: 30 minutes
Makes: 4 Servings

INGREDIENTS:
- 2 Italian-style chicken sausage links, cooked and thinly sliced
- 1 cup creamy Alfredo sauce
- ¼ cup Parmesan cheese, grated
- 1 garlic clove, chopped
- 1 ciabatta baguette, halved
- ¾ cup sliced mushrooms
- ¼ cup sliced black olives
- 1 ½ cup mozzarella, shredded
- 4 cup baby spinach
- 1 tbsp. fresh lemon juice
- 4 tbsp. olive oil
- ½ tsp. red pepper flakes

DIRECTIONS:
- Set the oven to 425 degrees.
- Start by mixing the chopped garlic, parmesan, and 3 tbsp. of olive oil together.
- Cut the ciabatta into four pieces.
- Place on the Copper Crisper cookie sheet.
- Top with the cheese mixture.
- Next, place the sausage links, mushrooms and black olives on top.
- Pour the cheese on top.
- Bake for 12 minutes.
- While baking, mix the spinach, lemon juice, olive oil, salt, pepper and red pepper flakes together
- Place the mixture on top.
- Serve immediately.

Cayenne Honey Herb Roasted Whole Chicken

Your home will start smelling like your favorite restaurant when you make this meal. Chicken has never tasted this good! You may have to start catering to those who want you to make this dish over and over again. Enjoy!

Total Time: 65 minutes
Makes: 4-6 Servings

INGREDIENTS:
- 1 large whole chicken
- 1/2 cup cooking oil (avocado or coconut oil for high heat)
- 1/4 cup water
- 1/2 teaspoon dried thyme
- 1/2 teaspoon dried oregano
- 1/2 teaspoon dried cayenne pepper
- 1 dash sea salt
- 1 dash pepper

DIRECTIONS:
- Preheat over to 350 degrees.
- Mix together the oil, water, salt, together in a bowl.
- Take your hands and rub the mix over the entire chicken. (helps keep moist)
- Wrap the chicken in foil and put it breast side down in the crisper basket.
- Make sure the foil will open at the top to keep juices locked in.
- Bake for about 35 minutes.
- Take the tray out of the oven remove the foil and turn chicken breast side up on the tray, brush with oil. Put the chicken back in the oven for about 20 min until golden brown.
- Mix the seasonings and honey together in small container till consistent.
- Take the chicken out brush or pour the honey mix over the chicken.
- Bake for another 10-15 min until glaze thickens...Yum!

By J. Martinez

Italian Style Cheesy Crusted Chicken

Mayonnaise spread on this dish gives it a sharp flavor that becomes the highlight of the chicken. Serve it with some spaghetti and a glass of white wine

Total Time: 30 minutes
Makes: 4 Servings

INGREDIENTS:
- 4 boneless, skinless chicken breast halves
- ½ cup Mayonnaise
- ¼ cup Parmesan cheese, grated
- 4 tsp. Italian seasoned bread crumbs
- 1 tsp. fresh parsley, chopped

DIRECTIONS:
- Set the oven to 425 degrees.
- Start with mixing the cheese, parsley and mayonnaise in a bowl.
- Place the chicken on the Copper Crisper cookie sheet and top with the mayonnaise mixture.
- Sprinkle the bread crumbs on top.
- Cook for 20 minutes.
- Serve and enjoy.
- Preheat oven to 425°.

Chicken Tenders Sub Sandwich

Cabbage and snap pea slaw is the star of this dish. Take the crunchiness of the chicken tenders and your got yourself a sandwich.

Total Time: 85 minutes
Makes: 8 Servings

INGREDIENTS:
- 1 ½ lb. chicken tenders
- 1 packet dry ranch dressing mix, divided
- 3 cup all-purpose flour
- 1 tbsp. baking powder
- 1 ½ cup buttermilk
- ¼ cup Greek Yogurt, plain
- 2 tbsp. Dijon mustard
- 1 16 oz. French bread loaf
- Cabbage and Snap Pea Slaw
- Salt to taste
- Pepper to taste

Cabbage Mix Ingredients
- 2 cups red cabbage, shredded
- 2 sugar snap peas, thinly sliced
- 1 large carrot, grated
- 1 large zucchini, grated
- ¼ cup parsley, torn
- 2 tsp. lemon zest
- 2 tsp. lemon juice
- 2 tbsp. olive oil
- Salt to taste
- Ground pepper to taste

DIRECTIONS:
- Set the oven to 350 degrees
- Mix the chicken with 2 tbsp. of the dressing mix in a bowl.
- In a separate bowl, mix the baking powder, 1 tsp salt and pepper, the

- remainder of the dressing mix and flour together.
- Add the buttermilk in a third bowl.
- Dip the chicken pieces in each bowl separately. Place in the flour mixture again and let sit for 10 minutes.
- Place the chicken in the Copper Crisper Tray .
- Cook for 30 minutes.
- Next, mix together mustard and yogurt in a bowl, along with salt and pepper.
- In another bowl, toss the cabbage, snap peas, sugar, carrot, dill, lemon juice, salt, pepper, and olive oil together. Let stand for 5 minutes.
- Cut the bread in half and spread the yogurt mixture evenly on both slices.
- Top with chicken and slaw.
- Place the top piece on top.
- Slice and serve.

Chicken and Pancakes

We have all heard of chicken and waffles, but chicken and pancakes is not something we hear about every day. Well, once you taste these cornbread pancakes, with tabasco style syrup and cayenne crusted chicken tenders, you will be saying Chicken and pancakes before chicken and waffles.

Total Time: 85 minutes
Makes: 4 Servings

INGREDIENTS:

- *Cornbread Pancakes*
- *1 ¾ cup yellow cornmeal*
- *1 ½ cup all-purpose flour*
- *4 ¼ tsp. sugar*
- *1 ½ tsp. baking powder*
- *3.4 tsp. baking soda*
- *¾ tsp. salt*
- *1 1.2 cup buttermilk*
- *6 eggs*
- *¼ cup buttermilk*
- *¼ cup unsalted butter, melted*

Chicken fingers
- *2 ½ cup all-purpose flour*
- *3 ¾ tsp. baking powder*
- *1 ¼ onion powder*
- *¾ tsp. cayenne pepper*
- *2 tsp. salt*
- *1 tsp. pepper*
- *1 ½ cup buttermilk*
- *1 ½ lb. chicken tenderloins*

Spicy syrup
- *1 cup pure maple syrup*
- *1 tsp. tabasco hot sauce*
- *½ tsp. pepper*
- *¼ tsp. salt*

By J. Martinez

DIRECTIONS:

- Start by making the pancakes: Mix the baking powder, baking soda, salt, sugar, flour and cornmeal together in a bowl.
- In a separate bowl, beat the eggs, buttermilk and butter together and then pour the liquid mixture into the dry mixture.
- Set the oven to 425 degrees
- Pour the mixture into the Copper Crisper cookie tray.
- Bake for ten minutes.
- Cut into squares, place on a separate plate and set aside.
- Next, to make the chicken fingers: Mix together the baking powder, flour, cayenne powder, salt, pepper and onion powder together.
- In two separate bowls, pour the eggs and buttermilk.
- Toss one piece of chicken at a time in the flour mixture, then the buttermilk and then the flour again.
- Leave the chicken in the flour mixture for 10 minutes.
- Place each of the pieces in the Copper Crisper Tray .
- Cook for 30 minutes.
- Set aside.
- To make the spicy syrup: mix the tabasco, pepper, salt and maple syrup in a microwave safe bowl.
- Microwave for 1 minute.
- Cool for 5 minutes.
- Serve the chicken on top of the pancakes and pour the syrup on top.

Chicken Rollatini

Rolled chicken stuffed with cheese? How could we ever go wrong with this recipe? The richness of the marinara sauce completes the meal.

Total Time: 35 minutes
Makes: 4 Servings

INGREDIENTS:
- ½ cup whole mike ricotta
- 4 oz. frozen spinach, thawed and excess water removed
- 2 tbsp. grated pecorino cheese
- 1 lb. thin-sliced chicken breasts
- 2 cup all-purpose flour
- 2 eggs, whisked
- 2 cups seasoned Italian breadcrumbs
- Kosher salt to taste
- Freshly ground black pepper to taste
- Marinara sauce to taste

DIRECTIONS:
- Set the oven temperature to 400 degrees.
- Start with mixing the ricotta, spinach and pecorino together.
- Lay the chicken cutlets on a cutting board and season with salt and pepper.
- Spread a tbsp. of the cheese mixture on each piece of chicken and roll it.
- Secure the chicken with toothpicks.
- Dip the chicken in the flour, the egg, and then the breadcrumbs.
- Place each in the Crisper Tray and bake for 35 minutes or until crispy and done.
- Serve with marinara sauce.

By J. Martinez

Oven Style Extra Crispy Fried Chicken

Eating fried chicken without the guilt. Your taste buds will never know the difference.

Total Time: 60 minutes
Makes: 4 Servings

INGREDIENTS:
- 2 chicken drumsticks
- 2 chicken thighs
- 1 qt. buttermilk
- 2 cups all-purpose flour
- 1 tbsp. smoked paprika
- 1 tbsp. salt
- 1 tsp. ground black pepper
- 1 tsp. chili powder

DIRECTIONS:
- Set the oven temperature to 375 degrees.
- Start with combining the buttermilk and chicken in a bowl.
- Marinate in the fridge for an hour.
- Mix the flour and the spices in another bowl.
- Take the chicken out of the fridge and smother with the flour mixture.
- Place the chicken in the Crisper Tray and cook for 30 minutes on each side.
- Remove when done.
- Serve with mashed potatoes and dipping sauces. Enjoy.

Hot & Tangy Chicken Wings

A new and crisper way to make wings without the sogginess. The hot and tangy will make this a go to snack any time of the year.

Total Time: 2 hours and 12 minutes
Makes: 4 Servings

INGREDIENTS:
- 2 lbs. chicken wings
- 3 tbsp. butter, melted
- ¼ cup hot sauce
- Salt to taste

Finishing Sauce
- 3 tbsp. butter, melted
- ¼ cup hot sauce

DIRECTIONS:
- Start by cutting the wing tips off the chicken and throw them away.
- Divide the drums from the wings and place in a bowl.
- Add the butter and hot sauce into the bowl.
- Marinate the wings for 2 hours.
- Set the oven temperature at 400 degrees.
- Place the wings in the Crisper Tray
- Bake for 12 minutes.
- Mix the butter and hot sauce while the wings are cooking.
- Serve with the remaining sauce and blue cheese for dipping. Enjoy.

By Elana Cordova

Boneless Chicken Tenders

This little treat will have your kids smiling. Add different dripping sauces and you will be the best mommy in the world.

Total Time: 15 minutes
Makes: 4 Servings

INGREDIENTS:
- 3 lb. boneless, skinless chicken breasts cut into even slices, about 5 per breast
- Onion powder, for seasoning
- 3 eggs
- ¼ milk
- 1 tbsp. vegetable oil
- ¼ cup flour
- 2 cups flour
- 1 tbsp. creole or Cajun seasoning
- 1 tbsp. garlic powder
- 1 tbsp. salt

DIRECTIONS:
- Set the oven temperature to 385 degrees.
- Start with slicing the chicken into small pieces.
- Season with garlic, onion, and creole seasoning.
- Add the flour, creole seasoning, salt, and garlic powder in one bowl.
- Mix the eggs, flour, milk and oil in another bowl.
- Place the chicken tenders in the Crisper Tray .
- Bake for 15 minutes.
- Remove from the oven and sprinkle with salt and creole seasoning.
- Serve with honey mustard and enjoy.

Paprika Glazed Turkey Breast

This is not your average thanksgiving turkey. The olive oil and glaze will give so much moisture to this bird that no one will ever complain about your turkey being dry again.

Total Time: 47 minutes
Makes: 4 Servings

INGREDIENTS:
- 2 tsp. olive oil
- 5 lb. whole turkey breast
- 1 tsp. dried thyme
- ½ tsp. dried sage
- ½ smoked paprika

DIRECTIONS:
- Set the oven temperature to 350 degrees.
- Start by rubbing oil all over the turkey breast.
- Mix the thyme, sage, paprika, salt and rub in a bowl.
- Rub the mixture all over the turkey breast.
- Place the turkey breast in the Crisper Tray .
- Bake for 25 minutes.
- Remove the turkey breast; turn the breast on its side and bake for another
  12-15 minutes.
- Combine the maple syrup, butter and mustard in a saucepan.
- Brush the glaze over the turkey when it is done, and let it cook for another 5 minutes.
- Let rest for 5 minutes.
- Serve and enjoy.

By J. Martinez

Oven Fried Lemon Rotisserie Chicken

Want to try something new for dinner this week? The tanginess of the lemon and the easiness of the recipe will have you adding this recipe to your weekly dinner list.

Total Time: 60 minutes
Makes: 4 Servings

INGREDIENTS:
- *6 lb. whole chicken*
- *2 tbsp. olive oil*
- *1 tbsp. seasoning salt*
- *1 whole lemon, forked everywhere*

DIRECTIONS:
- Set the oven temperature to 375 degrees.
- Start with washing the chicken and pat it dry with paper towels.
- Insert the lemon inside the chicken.
- Rub with olive oil, and seasoning salt.
- Place the chicken in the Crisper Tray, skin side down.
- Bake for 30 minutes.
- Flip over and bake for another 30 minutes.
- Let rest for 10 minutes.
- Serve and enjoy.

CRISPY But Juicy Baked Chicken Parm

This dish is easy and quick to make. The best part is you get all the chicken parm taste without the fat from frying.

Total Time: 35 minutes
Makes: 6

INGREDIENTS:
- ¾ cup plain breadcrumbs
- ½ teaspoon Italian seasoning
- ¼ teaspoon garlic powder
- 6 boneless skinless chicken breasts
- 1 egg beaten
- 1 jar marina sauce
- 1 cup shredded mozzarella cheese

DIRECTIONS
- Preheat your oven to 350 f.
- Mix together the seasoning, garlic powder, and breadcrumbs in a dish. Dip the chicken in the egg and then the breadcrumb mixture. Place the chicken in your crisper.
- Bake the chicken for 20 minutes. Then coat with marina and top with cheese, and bake for 10 additional minutes.
- Serve immediately with pasta if desired.

By J. Martinez

Baked Lemon Thyme Chicken Wings

These wings have a great citrus flavor that mixes well with the woodsy flavor of the thyme. The best part is there's very little prep time.

Total time: 35 minutes
Makes: 8

INGREDIENTS:
- 4 pounds chicken wings, cut in half at joint (wing tips removed)
- 1/4 cup fresh lemon juice
- 1 tablespoon ground pepper
- 1 tablespoon garlic powder
- 1 tablespoon onion powder
- 2 teaspoons coarse salt
- 2 teaspoons dried thyme crushed
- 1/2 teaspoon cayenne pepper
- 1/4 cup (1/2 stick) unsalted butter, melted
- Blue cheese or ranch dressing, or barbecue sauce, for dipping

DIRECTIONS
- Preheat your oven to 500 f.
- Toss the lemon juice and chicken in a big bowl. Then mix in the pepper, thyme, salt and pepper, garlic powder, and onion powder. Then mix in the butter and cayenne.
- Place the chicken wings in your crisper in a single layer. Bake the chicken for 30 minutes.
- Serve immediately with sauce of your choice.

Baked Spicy Garlic Ranch Chicken Strips

These strips are packed with flavor. The ranch makes them tangy, the cayenne gives them heat, and the garlic gives them a nice aromatic flavor.

Total Time: 55 minutes
Makes: 3-4

INGREDIENTS:
- *12 chicken tenders*
- *1 cup ranch dressing*
- *1 tbsp. milk*
- *1 cup complete baking mix*
- *1/2 tsp paprika*
- *1/2 tsp salt*
- *1/2 tsp black pepper*
- *1/2 teaspoon cayenne pepper*
- *2 garlic cloves minced*
- *Blue cheese or ranch dressing, or barbecue sauce, for dipping*

DIRECTIONS
- Preheat your oven to 475 f.
- Put the chicken and ranch in a large resealable plastic bag and shake it until the chicken is completely coated. Refrigerate the chicken for 30 minutes.
- Place the remaining ingredient in another large resealable plastic bag and then add in the chicken. Shake the bag until the chicken is fully coated with the seasoning.
- Put the chicken in your crisper in a single layer, and bake for 20 minutes, or until baked through.
- Serve immediately with dipping sauce of your choice.

By J. Martinez

LAMB:

Dijon Mustard Crusted Rack Of Lamb

Mustard and lamb go together like mint jelly. The breadcrumbs and lemon zest will make your mouth water, and help this recipe win a place as a traditional family dinner.

Total Time: 20 minutes
Makes: 4 Servings

INGREDIENTS:
- *1 rack of lamb*
- *1 tbsp. Dijon mustard*
- *¼ cup panko breadcrumbs*
- *2 tbsp. fresh herbs, chopped*
- *1/8 cup grated parmesan*
- *Zest of 1 lemon*
- *1 tbsp. olive oil*
- *Salt to taste*
- *Freshly ground black pepper to taste*

DIRECTIONS:
- Set the oven temperature to 375 degrees.
- Rub mustard all over the lamb.
- Mix the herbs, breadcrumbs, parmesan, lemon zest, and seasoning in a bowl.
- Season the lamb with the mixture.
- Place in the Crisper Tray .
- Roast for 20 minutes then serve and enjoy.

PORK:

Ranch Style Pork Chops

Ranch style pork chops served with potatoes is an easy recipe that can be made on a cookie sheet. Not only is it tasty, but it is easy for clean up as well

Total Time: 45 minutes
Makes: 6 Servings

INGREDIENTS:
- 6 boneless pork chops
- 1 oz. ranch salad dressing
- 1 oz. package ranch seasoning mix
- 3 tbsp. olive oil
- 1 ¼ tbsp. dry oregano
- 1 ¼ tsp. pepper
- 1 tbsp. parsley, chopped
- 2 lb. red baby potatoes

DIRECTIONS:
- Set the oven to 450 degrees.
- Place the pork chops and potatoes on the Copper Crisper cookie sheet.
- Pour olive oil on the pork chops and potatoes.
- Toss to coat.
- Next, mix the ranch dressing, ranch seasoning packet, paprika, pepper and oregano together.
- Rub the mixture over the pork chops and potatoes.
- Cook for 45 minutes.
- Sprinkle the parsley on top.
- Serve and enjoy.

By J. Martinez

Ham And Cheese Turnover

Turnovers often are paired with apples, or chocolate. But, what about ham and cheese? The gooiness of the cheese, with the bite of the ham will pair nicely in this crust pocket.

Total Time: 60 minutes
Makes: 4 Servings

INGREDIENTS:
- *3 russet potatoes, peeled and cut*
- *3 tbsp. unsalted butter*
- *¼ lb. baked ham, chopped*
- *½ medium onion, chopped*
- *¼ cup corn, frozen*
- *½ cup cheddar cheese, shredded*
- *1 tbsp. chives, chopped*
- *1 package puff pastry, thawed and halved*
- *Salt to taste*
- *Pepper to taste*

DIRECTIONS:
- Set the oven to 425 degrees.
- Pour 2 tsp. of salt, potatoes, and enough cold water to cover the potatoes in a large pot. Boil potatoes and let simmer for 25 minutes, until tender.
- Drain the potatoes and pour back into the pot.
- Next, add the butter, ham, onion, corn, chives, ¾ tsp. salt, and ¼ tsp. pepper.
- Mash well.
- Pour the mixture evenly on each of the puff pastry halves. Fold and seal.
- Place each turnover on the Crisper cookie sheet and cook for 30 minutes.
- Remove and serve.

Sweet And Savory Bacon Wrapped Pork Tenderloin

Everything tastes better with bacon. This bacon wrapped tenderloin will have your mouth watering as you fulfill your double pork craving.

Total Time: 60 minutes
Makes: 4 Servings

INGREDIENTS:
- 1 1 lb. pork tenderloin
- 1 tsp. steak seasoning
- 3 bacon slices, cut in half crosswise
- 1 tsp. brown sugar

DIRECTIONS:
- Set the oven to 400 degrees
- Place the bacon on the Copper Crisper cookie sheet
- Bake for 18 minutes and set aside.
- Mix the seasoning salt and brown sugar together.
- Rub the mixture onto the pork tenderloin on, on all sides.
- Wrap each piece of bacon around the tenderloin and secure it with toothpicks.
- Place the tenderloin in the Copper Crisper Tray and cook for 30 minutes.
- Remove and serve with rice and vegetables.

By J. Martinez

Bacon Bread Garlic Rolls

Everyone will be crazy about these bacon bread rolls at your next dinner party. You might want to make more than one batch because they will disappear fast.

Total Time: 45 minutes
Makes: 5 Servings

INGREDIENTS:
- *1/3 cup finely chopped onion*
- *1 tbsp. butter*
- *3 cups cubed day old bread*
- *¼ tsp. celery salt*
- *¼ tsp. garlic salt*
- *¼ tsp. garlic powder*
- *1/8 tsp. salt*
- *1.8 tsp. pepper*
- *1 large egg, lightly beaten*
- *10 bacon strips*

DIRECTIONS:
- Start by sautéing the onion in butter, until tender.
- Mix the bread crumbs, garlic powder, salt, pepper, celery salt and sautéed onions together. Mix evenly.
- Next, add the egg and mic together evenly.
- Make 10 balls.
- Wrap each piece of bacon on each dough ball. Secure in place with a toothpick.
- Set the oven to 350 degrees
- Place each bacon roll on the Copper Crisper cookie sheet and cook for 18 minutes, until the bacon is crispy.
- Serve and enjoy.

Fried Cornflake Bacon

Tender bacon with a little crispy crunch sounds like a treat any time of the day.

Total Time: 45 minutes
Makes: 9 Servings

INGREDIENTS:
- ½ cup milk, evaporated
- 2 ¼ tbsp. ketchup
- 1 tbsp. honey
- 1 tbsp. Worcestershire sauce
- 1 tsp. pepper
- 1 lb. bacon
- 3 cups crushed cornflakes
-

DIRECTIONS:
- Set the oven to 375 degrees.
- Mix the ketchup, pepper, milk and Worcestershire sauce together.
- Add the bacon strips and coat them in the mixture.
- Dip the bacon in the cornflakes and make sure that the flakes have been evenly dispersed.
- Place the bacon evenly on the Copper Crisper cookie sheet.
- Cook for 30 minutes.
- Serve and enjoy.

By J. Martinez

Toasted Coconut And Chocolate Baked Bacon

You can never go wrong with chocolate. Coating it with chocolate and coconut makes it ten times better.

Total Time: 40 minutes
Makes: 12 Servings

INGREDIENTS:
- *12 thick sliced bacon strips*
- *6 oz. white candy coating, coarsely chopped*
- *Toasted coconut to taste*
- *Chopped pecans to taste*
- *1 cup semisweet chocolate chips*
- *1 tbsp. shortening*

DIRECTIONS:
- Set the oven to 400 degrees.
- Place the bacon strips on the Copper Crisper cookie sheet and bake for 18 minutes.
- Let the bacon cool.
- Melt the candy coating in the microwave.
- Stir the coating until it is smooth and brush it on both sides of the bacon strips.
- Next, melt the chocolate chips and shortening until smooth and brush it on both sides of the bacon strips.
- Sprinkle with toppings as desired.
- Place on the cookie sheet and cool in fridge until it sets.
- Serve and enjoy.

Sweet Cream Cheese Stuffed Jalapenos

This is not your normal stuffed jalapeno. This particular appetizer paired with the crunchiness of the bacon, the additional gooiness with the cheddar cheese, the sweetness of the brown sugar and the spiciness of the chili will dazzle your taste buds.

Total Time: 30 minutes
Makes: 12 Servings

INGREDIENTS:
- *6 jalapeno peppers*
- *4 oz. cream cheese, softened*
- *2 tbsp. cheddar cheese, shredded*
- *¼ cup brown sugar*
- *¼ cup honey*
- *1 tbsp. chili seasoning mix*

DIRECTIONS:
- Set the oven at 350 degrees.
- Start with cutting the jalapenos in half, and remove the seed. Set aside.
- Combine the cheeses in bowl until blended.
- Put an even amount of the mixture into the pepper halves and wrap a half strip of bacon around each of the pepper halves.
- Mix the brown sugar and chili together and coat the pepper halves with the mixture.
- Place each on the Copper Crisper Cookie sheet and cook for 19 minutes.
- Serve and enjoy.

By J. Martinez

Bacon Wrapped Provolone Cheese Stuffed Dates

Enjoy this new date dish with cheese and bacon. We promise you will never look at a date the same again.

Total Time: 18 minutes
Makes: 6 Servings

INGREDIENTS:
- *24 dates, pitted*
- *2 oz. provolone cheese, cut into small rectangles*
- *8 slices bacon, cut into thirds*
- *¼ cup barbeque sauce*
- *Additional barbeque sauce for serving*

DIRECTIONS:
- Set the oven temperature to 400 degrees.
- Start with slicing the dates on one side.
- Place the cheese inside the date and wrap with the bacon.
- Secure the date with a toothpick.
- Drop the dates on the Crisper Tray Tray.
- Bake for 15 minutes.
- Remove after 15 minutes and brush with the barbeque sauce.
- Cook for another 3 minutes.
- Serve with barbeque sauce and enjoy.

Bacon Stuffed Mushrooms

Mushrooms stuffed with cream cheese and spinach makes for a great side or main dish.

Total Time: 20 minutes
Makes: 4 Servings

INGREDIENTS:
- *24- 28 medium white stuffer mushrooms*
- *1 8 oz. cream cheese, softened at room temperature*
- *1 small bag frozen spinach, thawed and drained*
- *6 bacon strips, cooked and crumbed*
- *1 cup grated cheddar cheese*

DIRECTIONS:
- Set the oven temperature to 350 degrees.
- Wash the mushrooms with a towel.
- Cut off the stems and set aside.
- Chop the stems and grills. Set aside.
- Mix the cream cheese, spinach, the stems, grills and bacon bits into a bowl.
- Place the filling into the mushroom caps and top with the cheddar cheese.
- Pour the mushrooms into the Crisper Tray .
- Bake for 20 minutes.
- Serve and Enjoy.

By J. Martinez

Ham Rolled Prawns

We have heard of bacon wrapped shrimp, but what about ham wrapped shrimp? Here is a little play on a great dish because everything tastes better with pork.

Total Time: 25 minutes
Makes: 4 Servings

INGREDIENTS:
- *1 large bell pepper, halved*
- *10 king prawns, defrosted*
- *5 slices of ham, raw*
- *1 tbsp. olive oil*
- *1 large garlic clove, crushed*
- *½ tbsp. paprika*
- *Freshly ground black pepper to taste*

DIRECTIONS:
- Set the oven temperature to 435 degrees.
- Place the red pepper in the Crisper Tray .
- Bake for 10 minutes.
- Remove from the oven and let rest for 10 minutes.
- Peel and devein the prawns.
- Slice the ham in half, wrap around each prawn, and coat with olive oil.
- Place the prawns in the Crisper Tray .
- Bake for 10 minutes.
- Peel the skin off the bell peppers, deseed and cut into pieces.
- Puree the bell peppers in the blender with garlic, paprika and olive oil.
- Pour the sauce in another dish and season with salt and pepper.
- Serve the prawns with the dip and enjoy.

Herb Crusted Pork Chops

Pork chops with pineapple salsa give a tropical flavor to a plain and dull dish

Total Time: 3 hours and 30 minutes
Makes: 3-4 Servings

INGREDIENTS:
3-4 pork chops, cut 1 inch thick
1 Jalapeno (2 for added heat)
1 tbsp. parsley, finely chopped
1 tbsp. cilantro, finely chopped
1 can crushed pineapple
1 tsp. garlic powder
1 tsp. olive oil
1 tsp. lemon juice
1 ½ tsp. salt

Marinade:
- *2 tsp. soy sauce (low sodium)*
- *2 tsp. Worcestershire sauce*
- *¼ cup olive oil*
- *1 tbsp. rosemary, finely chopped*
- *1 tbsp. Dijon mustard*
- *1 tbsp. ground coriander*
- *1 ½ tsp. sugar*

DIRECTIONS:
- Start with combing all of the marinade ingredients in a re-sealable bag.
- Put the pork chops in the bag and put in the fridge for 3 hours.
- Remove the pork chops from the fridge and sit them out for 20 minutes.
- Set the oven temperature to 375 degrees while pork chops are sitting.
- Brush the jalapenos with olive oil and place them in the Crisper Basket.
- Cook these first for 7-10 minutes while pork chops are sitting.
- Peel, seed and chop when they are cooled.
- Now, put the marinated pork chops in the basket.

- Cook for 20-25 minutes until done.
- Add the jalapenos, parsley, cilantro, pineapple, garlic powder, olive oil, lemon juice and salt together in a bowl and mix it all together.
- Serve this over the pork chops and enjoy.

Oven Fried Style Bacon

The smell of bacon frying on the stove on Saturday mornings. We can never go wrong/ now, we can have the same taste without all the fat.

Total Time: 18 minutes
Makes: 4 Servings

INGREDIENTS:
- *1 package of Applewood Smoked Bacon*

DIRECTIONS:
- Set the oven temperature to 400 degrees.
- Place each slide of bacon on the Crisper Tray Tray.
- Bake for 18 minutes.
- Serve and enjoy.

By J. Martinez

Honey Dijon Pigs In A Blanket With Tangy Mustard Sauce

These are an easy appetizer to make or the perfect finger food when you're using the BBQ. They've got a delicious depth of flavor thanks the mustard.

Total Time: 30 minutes
Makes: 4-6

INGREDIENTS:
- 1 8 ounce can of crescent rolls

- **Mustard sauce:**
- ¼ cup Dijon mustard
- ½ cup sour cream
- 20 mini hot dogs or cocktail franks
- ½ cup mayonnaise
- 1 egg, lightly beaten
- 3 tablespoons Dijon mustard
- 1 tablespoon whole-grain
- Mustard

DIRECTIONS
- Preheat your oven to 350f.
- Slice each piece of dough into 3 equal pieces lengthwise.
- Lightly coat the dough with the Dijon with a brush, and place a hot dog in each piece of dough. Make sure the hot dogs are put on one side of the dough and roll the dough around the hot dogs.
- Place the rolled up hot dogs in your crisper. Make sure the seam side is down, and brush with the beaten egg. Add poppy seeds or sesame seeds to the top if desired.
- Bake for around 12-15 minutes. They will be golden brown when ready.
- While the pigs in a blanket are cooking, mix all the dip ingredients in a bowl. Refrigerate the dip until it's time to serve the pigs in a blanket.
- Serve the pigs in a blanket hot.

Garlic Flavored Bacon Cheesey Fries

There's nothing better than French fries, except when you add bacon and cheese. The best part is there's no oil used so they're healthier

Total Time: 30 minutes
Servings: 3

INGREDIENTS
- *3 strips cooked bacon*
- *½ cup shredded cheese*
- *1 package frozen fries*
- *1 tbsp. Garlic powder*

DIRECTIONS
- Preheat your oven to 400 f.
- Put the fries in a single layer in the crisper and bake for 15-20 minutes. They will be golden brown when finished
- Preheat your broiler
- Sprinkle the cheese on the fries and top with bacon. Sprinkle the garlic powder over the top of the cheese. Broil for 1-2 minutes until the cheese melts.
- Serve immediately.

By Elana Cordova

Baked Adobo Lime Steak Fajitas

Adobo is a Puerto Rican seasoning mix that is packed with exotic flavor. It pairs well with the citrus flavor with the lime.

Total Time: 55 minutes
Makes: 3-4

INGREDIENTS:
- 1 lb. Thin sirloin steak, slice in 1/4 inch strips
- 1 white onion sliced
- 1 red bell pepper, sliced
- 1 green bell pepper, sliced
- 1 tbsp. oil
- 3 tsp adobo
- Juice from 2 limes
- Flour or white corn tortillas

DIRECTIONS
- Preheat your oven to 400 f.
- Place the oil, adobo, and lime juice in a bowl and mix well. Then toss the steak and vegetable in the mixture
- Place the ingredient in your crisper in a single layer. Bake for 20 minutes
- Serve immediately with tortillas

FISH:

Scallops With Brown Sugar Pear Sauce

Bacon wrapped scallops is a wonderful dish, but this pear dipping sauce will be a great additional to this already amazing dish.

Total Time: 40 minutes
Makes: 12 Servings

INGREDIENTS:
- 12 bacon strips
- ¾ cup pear preserves
- 2 tbsp. soy sauce
- 1 ¼ tbsp. brown sugar
- ½ tsp. red pepper flakes, crushed
- 12 sea scallops
- 1 ¼ tsp. olive oil
- 1/8 tsp. salt
- 1/8 tsp. pepper

DIRECTIONS:
- Set the oven to 375 degrees.
- Place the bacon on the Copper Crisper cookie tray and slightly cook for 7 minutes. Set aside on paper towels and keep warm.
- Next, mix the pear preserves, soy sauce, brown sugar and pepper flakes in a saucepan. Bring to a boil, then reduce the heat and simmer for 5 minutes.
- Wrap a bacon strip around each of the scallops and secure with a toothpick.
- Season with salt and pepper.
- Place each of the scallops in the Copper Crisper Tray.
- Cook for 15 minutes. Serve with the pear sauce and enjoy.

By J. Martinez

Sautéed Halibut With Bacon Scallions

The Cajun seasoning of the fish brings a little heat with this dish. Served with the bacon corn dish completes it well. Yum!

Total Time: 60 minutes
Makes: 4 Servings

INGREDIENTS:
- 4 6 oz. halibut fillets
- 2 tsps. Cajun seasoning
- 4 slices bacon
- 4 scallions, sliced with white and green parts separated
- 2 cups corn
- 2 cups peas
- ½ head of cabbage, cut into strips
- 2 tbsp. cider vinegar
- Salt to taste
- Pepper to taste

DIRECTIONS:
- Set the oven to 450 degrees.
- Place the fish in the Copper Crisper Tray .
- Sprinkle the Cajun seasoning on top.
- Cook for 12 minutes until opaque.
- Next, cook the bacon in a skillet for 7 minutes.
- Set aside on a towel and break into pieces after it has cooled.
- Cook the scallions in the bacon grease for 3 minutes.
- Then add the cabbage, corn, salt, pepper, and cook for another 5 minutes.
- Lastly, add the vinegar and green parts of the scallion mixing well.
- Sprinkle the bacon on top and serve with the fish.

Copper Tray Style Salmon Cakes

Dill sauce, lemon, tuna and Dijon mustard are all paired together in a tangier version of these salmon cakes.

Total Time: 75 minutes
Makes: 4 Servings

INGREDIENTS:
- *1 ½ extra-virgin olive oil*
- *1 small onion, chopped*
- *1 stalk celery, finely diced*
- *2 tbsp. fresh parsley, chopped*
- *15 oz. canned salmon, drained*
- *1 egg, beaten*
- *1 ½ tsp. Dijon mustard*
- *1 3/4 breadcrumbs*
- *½ tsp. ground pepper*
- *½ tsp. salt*
- *1 lemon, wedged*
- *Creamy dill sauce for dipping*

DIRECTIONS:
- Set the oven to 450 degrees.
- Start with heating the oil in a nonstick pan on medium heat.
- Add in the celery and the onion and cook for 3 minutes until soft.
- Stir in parsley and remove.
- Next, put the salmon in a bowl and flake apart with a fork. Make sure you remove any skin and bones.
- Now, add the egg, and mustard. Mix well.
- Pour in the onion mixture, breadcrumbs and pepper.
- Shape the salmon mixture into 8 patties.
- Add the patties to the Copper Crisper cookie sheet.
- Cook for 8 minutes.
- While cooking, prepare the dill sauce
- Serve the tuna patties with the dill sauce and lemon wedges.

By J. Martinez

Cheesy Baked Tuna Cakes

This is a play on a modern classic – the infamous tuna melt. Bread crumbs replacing the sandwich slices; give you the same taste you love without all the carbs.

Total Time: 45 minutes
Makes: 12 Servings

INGREDIENTS:
- *2 eggs*
- *2 cans chunk light tuna in water, drained and flaked*
- *1 pkg. Stove Top Stuffing Mix for Chicken*
- *1 cup water*
- *1 stalk celery, finely chopped*
- *4 green onions, chopped*
- *Juice of 1 lemon*
- *1 tbsp. lemon pepper*
- *½ cup mayonnaise*
- *¼ lb. Velveeta cheese, cut into 12 cubes*

DIRECTIONS:
- Set the oven to 400 degrees.
- Start with mixing all of the ingredients, except the cheese together.
- Form the mixture into 12 balls.
- Place each ball on the Copper Crisper cookie sheet.
- Press 1 cheese cube in the middle of each tuna ball. Make sure to enclose in the middle of each ball.
- Cook for 15 minutes.
- Remove and let cool for 5 minutes.
- Serve and enjoy.

Oven Fried Fish Sandwiches

These fish sandwiches use Greek seasoning and lemon pepper to spice up the pallet to this usual mediocre dish. Since it is hand held you can use your hands because you are going to want to take it on the go with you.

Total Time: 24 minutes
Makes: 4 Servings

INGREDIENTS:
- *2 lbs. Mahi Mahi fillets*
- *2 tbsp. Greek Seasoning, divided*
- *2 tbsp. lemon pepper*
- *1 tsp. ground pepper*
- *2 ¼ cups all-purpose flour*
- *¼ cup yellow cornmeal*
- *2 tsp. baking powder*
- *2 cups cold beer*
- *1 egg, beaten*
- *4 sesame seed hamburger buns*
- *4 green leaf lettuce leaves*
- *4 tomato slices*
- *Tartar sauce to taste*

DIRECTIONS:
- Set the oven to 450 degrees.
- Start by cutting the fish into 3 – inch strips.
- Season with 1 tsp. Greek seasoning, 1 tsp. lemon pepper, 1 tsp. salt and ½ tsp. pepper.
- In a bowl, mix the flour, cornmeal, baking powder, remaining Greek seasoning,
- Cut fish into 3-inch strips. Sprinkle evenly with 1 tsp. Greek seasoning 1 tsp. Italian seasoning, 1 tsp. salt, and 1/2 tsp. pepper together.
- Now, add the beer and egg in the mixture until it is blended smoothly.
- Next, dip the fish into the batter by coating both sides.
- Place the fish in the Copper Crisper Tray . You might have to cook in batches.

- Cook for 15 minutes for each batch.
- Take the tartar sauce and spread evenly on each bun.
- Add 1 piece of lettuce and tomato slice on the bottom half of each bun.
- Top with 2 fried fish strips and add the top half.
- Serve and enjoy.

Cajun Style Catfish

This southern classic can be served in many different ways, but this way can be a zinger at your next family dinner or dinner party. Combining Worcestershire, paprika, parmesan cheese and Cajun seasoning is a nice addition to this dish.

Total Time: 22 minutes
Makes: 6 Servings

INGREDIENTS:
- 3 cups cornflakes, finely crushed
- ¾ cups Parmesan cheese, grated
- 1 ¼ tsp. paprika
- ½ tsp. salt
- ½ cup Mayonnaise
- 1 tsp. Worcestershire sauce
- 6 catfish fillets
- 1 ½ tsp. Cajun seasoning
- 3 tsp. Parsley, chopped
- Lemon wedges for garnish

DIRECTIONS:
- Set the oven to 350 degrees.
- Start with mixing together the cornflakes, parmesan cheese, paprika and salt together.
- Add the mayonnaise and Worcestershire sauce in a separate bowl.
- Spread the mayonnaise mixture onto the catfish fillets.
- Season the fish with ¼ of the Cajun seasoning on both sides of the fillets.
- Next, dip the fish in the cornflakes. Make sure that the mixture is even.
- Place the fillets in the Copper Crisper Tray .
- Cook for 15 minutes.
- Sprinkle with parsley, and lemon wedges.
- Serve and enjoy.

By J. Martinez

Crab Cakes

Crab meat, lemon juice, Dijon mustard and breadcrumbs. A taste of luxury in your mouth.

Total Time: 12 minutes
Makes: 8 Servings

INGREDIENTS:
- 1 lb. lump crab meat
- 3 scallions, chopped
- ½ red bell pepper, seeded and diced
- ½ green bell pepper, seeded and diced
- ¼ cup mayonnaise
- 2 eggs, beaten
- 1 tbsp. Worcestershire sauce
- 1 tsp. Dijon mustard
- 1 tsp. lemon juice
- 1 cup panko breadcrumbs
- ½ tsp. black pepper
- ½ tsp. salt
- Dill, for garnish

DIRECTIONS:
- Set the oven temperature to 350 degrees.
- Combine the scallions, bell peppers, mayonnaise, eggs, Worcestershire sauce, Dijon, lemon juice, panko, salt and pepper in a large bowl.
- Add the crabmeat and mix together.
- Form into 8 patties and pour into the Crisper Tray .
- Bake for 12 minutes and flip halfway through.
- Serve with dill and enjoy.

Oven Fried Coconut Shrimp

The joy of being able to cook Coconut Shrimp without being on the grill, and with the great taste of frying without the effects of the grease.

Total Time: 15 minutes
Makes: 4 Servings

INGREDIENTS:
- *12 large shrimp, raw*
- *1 cup egg white, raw*
- *1 cup coconut, dried and unsweetened*
- *1 tbsp. cornstarch*
- *1 cup panko bread crumbs*
- *1 cup white flour*

DIRECTIONS:
- Set the oven temperature to 350 degrees.
- Start with placing the shrimp on paper towels and set aside.
- Mix the panko crumbs and the coconut together in a pan. Also set aside.
- Stir the flour and cornstarch together. Set aside.
- Beat the eggs in another separate bowl.
- Dip the shrimp in the flour mix, egg whites, and then the coconut mixture.
- Pour the shrimp in the Crisper Tray .
- Cook for 15 minutes.
- Serve with ranch dressing and enjoy.

By J. Martinez

Tex-Mex Cod Fish Cakes With Salsa

The taste of Mexico inside your kitchen! The play on ingredients will make you feel like you are dining on the beach, and the only thing missing is a nice cold drink by your side.

Total Time: 7 minutes
Makes: 4 Servings

INGREDIENTS:
- 1 ripe mango
- 1 ½ tsp. red chili paste
- 3 tbsp. fresh coriander or flat leaf parsley
- Juice and zest of 1 lime
- 1 lb. cod
- 1 egg
- 1 green onion, finely chopped
- 1 ¾ cup ground coconut

DIRECTIONS:
- Set the oven temperature to 375 degrees.
- Peel the mango and cut into small pieces.
- Add the mango, red chili paste, coriander, and the lime together in a small bowl.
- Puree the fish and mix with the egg, salt, the remaining lime zest, red chili paste and lime juice.
- Separate the fish into 12 pieces.
- Shape them into cakes and coat with coconut.
- Pour in the Crisper Tray .
- Bake for 7 minutes.
- Serve with the salsa and enjoy.

Baked Cajun "Square Pan Fried" Fish Strips

This is a kicked up version of the fish from fish and chips. The Cajun seasoning, and the garlic add a world of flavor. Yum!

Total time: 25 minutes
Makes: 4 Servings

INGREDIENTS:
- 1 1/2 pounds skinless, boneless Pollock (or other firm white fish), cut into 2-by-4-inch pieces
- 2 3/4 cups crispy rice cereal, crushed
- 3 teaspoons Cajun seasoning
- 2 garlic clove finely minced
- Kosher salt
- Black pepper
- 3 large eggs

DIRECTIONS
- Preheat your oven to 450 f.
- Mix together the cereal, garlic, seasoning, and pepper in a bowl.
- Whisk the eggs with a pinch of salt, until the mixture becomes frothy.
- Dip the fish in the egg mixture and then the cereal mixture.
- Place the fish in your crisper and bake until the fish is cooked through, around 15 minutes.
- Serve immediately, with fries if desired.

By J. Martinez

VEGETARIAN:

Vegetarian Sesame Seed Spring Rolls

Ahhh... a little taste of the orient for ya! Vegetarian spring rolls made in your very own kitchen. Fast, easy and memorable.

Total Time: 15-20 minutes
Makes: 4 Servings

INGREDIENTS:
- Spring roll wrappers
- ½ cabbage, sliced in very thin strips
- 2 large carrots, grated on the coarse side
- A dash of soy sauce
- A few drops of sesame seed oil
- Optional egg noodles
- Optional toasted sesame seeds
- 100 ml vegetable oil
- 1 egg white, beaten

DIRECTIONS:
- Set the oven temperature to 385 degrees.
- Sauté the vegetables on very high heat for about 3-4 min.
- Add the soy sauce and sesame oil for seasoning.
- Let cool and add the sesame seeds.
- Place the wrappers down and brush with the egg whites.
- Place the vegetables in the wrapper and fold up the sides.
- Put in the Crisper Tray , folded side down.
- Repeat until the mix is used then brush the rolls with oil.
- Bake for 10 minutes and serve with sweet and sour sauce and enjoy.

Vegetarian Style Ravioli

Breaded ravioli? Italian food just keeps getting better and better.

Total Time: 12 minutes
Makes: 4 Servings

INGREDIENTS:
- *1 jar marinara sauce, store-bought*
- *1 box cheese ravioli, store-bought*
- *Olive oil*
- *2 cups Italian-style bread crumbs*
- *1 cup buttermilk*
- *¼ cup parmesan cheese*

DIRECTIONS:
- Set the oven temperature to 350 degrees.
- Start with dipping the ravioli in buttermilk.
- Add the oil to the breadcrumbs and roll the ravioli around in it.
- Place the ravioli in the Crisper Tray .
- Bake for 12 minutes.
- Serve and enjoy with parmesan cheese.

By J. Martinez

Eggplant Parmigiana Cakes

Want to be spontaneous in the kitchen? Here is a new way to cook a traditional dish. Even your grandmother would be pleased.

Total Time: 100 minutes
Makes: 4 Servings

INGREDIENTS:
- *3 medium eggplants, thinly sliced*
- *10 basil leaves, chopped*
- *15 Oz. basil leaves, chopped*
- *15 oz. ricotta cheese, drained of excess moisture*
- *1 cup mozzarella cheese*
- *½ cup parmesan cheese*
- *4 eggs, beaten*
- *1 cup Italian seasoned bread crumbs*
- *Salt to taste*
- *Marinara sauce for dipping*

DIRECTIONS:
- Set the oven temperature to 350 degrees.
- Start with slicing the eggplant and set out on a towel.
- Salt on both sides and let sit for 30 minutes.
- Mix the basil, cheeses, and one egg into a bowl.
- Sandwich the mixture in-between two slices and place on wax paper and freeze for 30 minutes.
- Coat the eggplant in each bowl in order (3 eggs in one bowl and breadcrumbs in the other) and place back in the freezer.
- Place all the patties in the basket.
- Bake for 40 minutes and serve with marinara sauce.

Melted Mozzarella Stuffed Onion Rings

You get double the delight with this recipe. They're a delicious combo of onion rings and mozzarella sticks.

Prep time: 1 hour 30 minutes
Cook time: 22 minutes
Servings: 3

INGREDIENTS:
- 1 large sweet onion, cut into 1/2 inch thick rings
- 2 1/2 cups buttermilk
- 12 sticks part skim mozzarella cheese sticks, frozen
- 1 cup whole wheat flour, divided ¾ cup and ¼ cup
- 3 large eggs beaten
- 1/2 cup cornmeal
- 1/2 cup panko
- 1/2 cup corn Chex or cornflakes, crushed
- 1/2 teaspoon kosher salt
- 1/4 teaspoon ground black pepper
- Marinara sauce or ranch dressing, for dipping

DIRECTIONS
- Put the onions and buttermilk in shallow container and refrigerate for a minimum of an hour. Make sure the onions are coated by the buttermilk.
- Preheat your oven to 425f. Use aluminum foil to line a baking sheet.
- Put the onions on the baking sheet. Place them in couples. Make sure that one onion is ½ smaller than the other. Place smaller one inside the larger one.
- Take the string cheese out of the freezer and let it soften for 5 minutes. Slice the cheese into quarters lengthwise. Put a piece of cheese in space between the two onions.
- Put ¾ cup flour in a small sized bowl. Have the eggs in a second bowl. Mix the remaining flour, panko, Chex, cornmeal, salt, and pepper in a third bowl.
- Dip onion rings in the pure flour bowl, then egg, then pure flour again, before putting it in the eggs again. Then dip onion rings in the seasoning bowl.
- Put onion rings in a single layer in your crisper. Bake around 22 minutes.
- Serve immediately with marinara or ranch if desired.

By J. Martinez

Spicy Maple Syrup Twice Baked Sweet Potatoes

These make a great side dish, or dessert. The cayenne gives a little heat to this sweet dish

Total time: 1 hour 35 minutes
Makes: 12 Servings:

INGREDIENTS:
- *9 sweet potatoes, about 12 ounces each*
- *1 tablespoon canola or vegetable oil*
- *1 stick (8 tablespoons) unsalted butter, cut into tablespoons*
- *1/3 cup pure maple syrup, ideally grade b*
- *3/4 teaspoon ground cinnamon*
- *Sea salt*
- *Cayenne pepper*
- *3 cups mini marshmallows*

DIRECTIONS
- Preheat your oven to 350 f.
- Use a fork to prick the sweet potatoes 5 or 6 times all over.
- Then bake them for around 1 hour. The will be tender when done.
- Allow the potatoes to cool a little. Then slice them in half lengthwise.
- Take out the flesh and put it in a saucepan. Keep 12 of the potato skins.
- Put the saucepan on medium heat, mash and whip the potatoes with a whisk for about 5 minutes.
- Add in the butter, maple syrup, cinnamon, cayenne, and salt. Continue to whisk until smooth & mixture is hot.
- Put the mixture in the 12 potato skins. Place them in your crisper, and push the marshmallows into the top of the potatoes.
- Bake for another 15 minutes, then turn on the broiler until the top of the marshmallows are browned, about 1 minutes.
- Serve immediately.

Parmesan Crusted Baked Zucchini

This makes a perfect appetizer or side dish. The parmesan gives these a nice crunch, and the oregano gives them a nice woodsy flavor.

Total time: 50 minutes
Makes: 4-6 Servings

INGREDIENTS:
- *2 medium zucchini sliced into 1/8 inch thick rounds*
- *2 tablespoons melted butter*
- *1 tablespoon fresh oregano*
- *1/4 cup grated parmesan cheese*

DIRECTIONS
- Preheat your oven to 350 f.
- Mix the zucchini with the butter and oregano.
- Place the zucchini in your crisper and top with parmesan.
- Bake for 40 minutes.
- Salt and pepper to taste.

By J. Martinez

Oven Baked Herb Potatoes

Garlic and parsley can help remake any dish. These potatoes are great to serve with a nice piece if steak, chicken, or by themselves.

Total Time: 40 minutes
Makes: 4 Servings

INGREDIENTS:
- *3 Idaho or Russet baking potatoes*
- *2 tbsp. olive oil*
- *1 tsp. salt*
- *1 tsp. garlic*
- *1 tsp. parsley*

DIRECTIONS:
- Set the oven temperature to 395 degrees.
- Start washing the potatoes and stab them a few times.
- Sprinkle with seasoning and olive oil.
- Place in the Crisper Tray .
- Bake for 40 minutes.
- Serve and enjoy.

Oven Fried Broccoli

Americans are famous for finding more ways to eat their vegetables. Covering with cheese, and now flour is another way to enjoy these little green treats.

Total Time: 25 minutes
Makes: 4 Servings

INGREDIENTS:
- 1 lb. broccoli flowerets
- 1 tbsp. flour

DIRECTIONS:
- Set the oven temperature to 400 degrees.
- Start with cutting the broccoli into small florets
- Soak in a bowl with water and salt.
- Remove and drain.
- Add of all of the marinade ingredients in a clean bowl.
- Cover and set in the fridge for 15 minutes.
- Pour the broccoli in the Crisper Tray .
- Bake for 10 minutes.
- Serve and enjoy.

By J. Martinez

Parmesan Roasted Corn On The Cob

Parmesan Roasted Corn on the cob is a celebrated dish at any table. The addition of butter and parmesan cheese are what makes this dish superior than the rest.

Total Time: 45 minutes
Makes: 4 Servings

INGREDIENTS:
- *4-6 pieces of corn on the cob*
- *Kosher salt to taste*
- *Fresh ground pepper to taste*
- *1 cup butter*
- *1 cup parmesan Cheese*

DIRECTIONS:
- Set the oven temperature to 400 degrees.
- Coat the corn with salt, pepper and parmesan cheese.
- Pour the corn into the Crisper Tray .
- Smear butter on the cobs and roast for 45 minutes.
- Add more butter if desired.
- Serve and enjoy.

Garlic Sweet Potato Fries

Sweet potatoes are what make this dish, not the garlic. Who needs regular potatoes when you have these?

Total Time: 40 minutes
Makes: 4 Servings

INGREDIENTS:
- *3 sweet potatoes*
- *½ cup olive oil*
- *½ cup garden powder*
- *½ cup parmesan cheese*
- *Sea salt to taste*
- *Freshly ground pepper to taste*

DIRECTIONS:
- Set the oven temperature to 400 degrees.
- Start with peeling the potatoes and cut into slices.
- Rinse them and pat dry with a towel.
- Place the potatoes in a bowl and drench with olive oil.
- Next, sprinkle with garlic powder, salt and pepper.
- Place them in the Crisper Tray .
- Bake for 20 minutes.
- Remove, stir and bake for another 20 minutes.
- Sprinkle with cheese.
- Serve and enjoy.

By J. Martinez

Roasted Onions And Peppers

Peppers and onions have always been vegetables we add to dishes, but they aren't often emphasized on their own. This recipe will show you how good these two ingredients can be by themselves.

Total Time: 25 minutes
Makes: 4 Servings

INGREDIENTS:
- 1 tbsp. olive oil
- 1 tbsp. Maggi
- 1 onion, small
- 12 bell peppers (3 red, green, yellow and orange)

DIRECTIONS:
- Set the oven temperature to 425 degrees.
- Combine the olive oil and Maggi in a bowl.
- Slice and peel the onion and add it to the bowl.
- Wash, cut, stem, seed and slice all of the peppers and add them to the bowl.
- Pour the mixture into the Crisper Tray .
- Cook for 25 minutes.
- Serve and enjoy.

Olive Oil Roasted Mushrooms

Who doesn't love mushrooms? There are so many ways to cook them, but with vermouth? Try this new recipe and you will not be disappointed.

Total Time: 30 minutes
Makes: 4 Servings

INGREDIENTS:
- 2 lbs. mushrooms
- 1 tbsp. olive oil
- ½ tsp. garlic powder
- 2 tsp. Herbs de Provence
- 2 tbsp. white vermouth, aka French

DIRECTIONS:
- Set the oven temperature to 350 degrees.
- Start by washing the mushrooms, dry and slice into quarters.
- Set aside.
- Pour the olive oil, garlic powder, and the herbs in a bowl.
- Add the mushrooms to the mixture.
- Next, add to the Crisper Tray .
- Cook for 25 minutes.
- Remove from the oven and add the vermouth.
- Cook for another 5 minutes.
- Serve and enjoy.

By Elana Cordova

Asparagus Style Fries

Did you ever imagine saying asparagus and fries in the same sentence? Me neither. These breaded delicacies will be the star at your next BBQ.

Total Time: 20 minutes
Makes: 4 Servings

INGREDIENTS:
- *20 pieces asparagus spears, hard ends taken away*
- *½ cup flour*
- *1 egg*
- *½ cup whole grain breadcrumbs*
- *1/3 cup parmesan cheese, grated*

DIRECTIONS:
- Set the oven temperature to 400 degrees.
- Rinse the tips of the asparagus and separate them from the bottoms.
- Place the asparagus in the flour, then the egg, and finally the breadcrumbs/
- Put them on the tray.
- Bake for 10 minutes.
- Remove from the oven and pour the cheese on top.
- Bake for another 10 minutes.
- Serve and enjoy.

Rosemary Roasted Red Potatoes

An easy way to cook potatoes and be the hit at the next family dinner.

Total Time: 53 minutes
Makes: 4 Servings

INGREDIENTS:
- 3 red potatoes
- 1 tsp. olive oil
- Pinch of sea salt to taste
- Freshly ground black pepper to taste
- Desired herbs to taste

DIRECTIONS:
- Set the oven temperature to 325 degrees.
- Rinse the potatoes under the tab and cut into quarters.
- Place the quarters into a large bowl and toss with a tsp. of olive oil, sea salt, pepper and herbs.
- Bake for 25 minutes.
- Remove from the oven and basket.
- Recoat with oil mixture.
- Place in the basket again and raise the temperature to 350 degrees.
- Bake for another 6-8 minutes.
- Repeat the process and cook for a final 7 minutes.
- Serve and enjoy.

By J. Martinez

Oven Roasted Vegetables

Want to come up with a new vegetable dish? Oven roast your vegetables with a squeeze of lemon juice to spruce them up.

Total Time: 30 minutes
Makes: 4 Servings

INGREDIENTS:
- *2 large carrots*
- *2 cups cauliflower*
- *2 cups Brussel sprouts*
- *1 tsp. olive oil*
- *1 lemon, juiced*
- *Pink salt to taste*
- *Freshly ground black pepper to taste*

DIRECTIONS:
- Set the oven temperature to 400 degrees.
- Wash and slice the vegetables into small chunks and place in a large bowl.
- Pour olive oil, salt, pepper, and herbs evenly on the vegetables.
- Place in the Crisper Tray .
- Bake for 15 minutes.
- Remove, stir and bake for another 15 minutes.
- Pour lemon juice on top.
- Serve and enjoy.

Crinkled Parsnips

Want to find a way to get you children to eat parsnips? Well, everyone loves fries. Make this dish a hit in your home.

Total Time: 25 minutes
Makes: 4 Servings

INGREDIENTS:
- *6 medium parsnips*
- *¼ cup cornstarch*
- *¼ cup olive oil*
- *1/3 cup water*
- *Salt to taste*

DIRECTIONS:
- Set the oven temperature to 400 degrees.
- Cut and peel the parsnips.
- Mix water, olive oil, cornstarch and the parsnips in a mixing bowl.
- Coat evenly.
- Place the parsnips in the Crisper Tray
- Cook for 25 minutes.
- Serve and enjoy.

By J. Martinez

Vegetable Pasta Salad

Pasta salad with roasted eggplant? It's different than any other pasta salad you have ever eaten before and will eat again. Make this the next salad you serve at your next party.

Total Time: 95 minutes
Makes: 4 Servings

INGREDIENTS:
- *3 small eggplants or one large*
- *2 tbsp. olive oil*
- *3 medium size zucchini*
- *4 medium tomatoes cut in eighths*
- *4 cups of shaped large pasta, uncooked*
- *2 bell peppers*
- *1 cup sliced cherry tomatoes*
- *2 tsp. salt*
- *8 tbsp. grated parmesan*
- *½ cup fat free Italian dressing*
- *Few leaves of fresh basil*

DIRECTIONS:
- Set the oven temperature to 350 degrees.
- Start with washing the eggplant and slice.
- Throw away the green end.
- Pour olive oil on top.
- Place in the Crisper Tray .
- Cook for 40 minutes.
- Set aside.
- Wash the slice the zucchini.
- Repeat the process.
- Cook for 25 minutes.
- Wash the tomatoes.
- Place in the basket.
- Cook for 30 minutes.
- Cook the pasta on the stove according to the package.

- Wash seed and chop the bell pepper.
- Add all of the vegetables with the pasta, salt, dressing, basil and parmesan together.
- Place in the fridge and marinade.
- Serve later and enjoy.

By J. Martinez

Cinnamon Sugar Sweet Potatoes

A healthier version to the French fry with a little cinnamon twist. The combination of salt and cinnamon will dance on your taste buds and have you asking why you have never eaten these fries before.

Total Time: 15 minutes
Makes: 6 Servings

INGREDIENTS:
- *2 large sweet potatoes*
- *2 tbsp. coconut oil or vegetable oil*
- *1 tsp. ground cinnamon*
- *½ tsp. salt*

DIRECTIONS:
- Set the oven temperature to 425 degrees.
- Cut the sweet potatoes into sticks and place them on the copper tray.
- Pour oil, cinnamon and salt on top each of the sticks.
- Bake for 15 minutes.
- Serve with maple syrup and enjoy.

Wedged Potato Chips

A play of two traditional dishes – potato chips and wedges. The tanginess of the paprika will be a hit, and something you want to keep in your cooking repertoire.

Total Time: 85 minutes
Makes: 4 Servings

INGREDIENTS:
- 4 medium russet potatoes
- 1 cup water
- 3 tbsp. canola oil
- 1 tsp. paprika
- ¼ tsp. black pepper
- ¼ tsp. salt

DIRECTIONS:
- Set the oven temperature to 390 degrees.
- Run the potatoes under water and scrub clean.
- Boil in salted water for 40 minutes
- Let cook for 30 minutes in the fridge.
- Add the canola oil, paprika, salt and pepper together in a mixing bowl.
- Cut the potatoes in quarters and toss in the bowl.
- Pour the potatoes in the Crisper Tray and place them skin down.
- Bake each batch for 15 minutes.
- Serve with ketchup and enjoy.

By J. Martinez

DESSERTS:

Golden S'more Cookies

S'mores reminds us of us of our childhood, colder days, and sitting around the campfire. Try this version without the hassle of making a fire.

Total Time: 85 minutes
Makes: 24 Servings

INGREDIENTS:
- *8 cups Teddy Graham's crackers*
- *1 1 Oz. bag (5 ½ cups)small marshmallows*
- *1 ¾ cups milk chocolate chips*
- *5: tbsp. butter*
- *¼ cup sugar*
- *1 tbsp. water*
- *1 tsp. vanilla*

DIRECTIONS:
- Start by pouring 4 ½ cups of marshmallows, butter, sugar, water and chocolate chips in a saucepan.
- Heat over low heat until melted and stir occasionally.
- Remove the pan from the hot burner and stir in the vanilla.
- Measure the Teddy grahams in another bowl.
- Stir in the mixture until coated evenly.
- Next, pour in and stir the remaining marshmallows
- Break dough apart into 24 cookies and place on the Copper Crisper cookie sheet.
- Cool for an hour until firm. Can refrigerate in desired. Serve and enjoy.

Chocolate Chip Pan Cookies

Something the kids will love, a big giant chocolate chip cookie. Who doesn't want to eat one of the world's biggest cookies?

Total Time: 15 minutes
Makes: 20Servings

INGREDIENTS:
- *1 cup brown sugar*
- *½ cup butter*
- *½ cup coffee, cold*
- *1 egg*
- *1 tsp. vanilla*
- *1 cup flour*
- *½ tsp. baking soda*
- *½ tsp. baking powder*
- *¼ tsp. salt*
- *1 tsp. cinnamon*
- *1 cup chocolate chips*

Icing
- *Sugar, powdered*

DIRECTIONS:
- First, preheat the oven to 350 degrees.
- Next, mix all of the ingredients into a large mixing bowl.
- Roll out the cookie dough onto the Copper Crisper cookie sheet.
- Let cook for 15 minutes.
- Sprinkle sugar on top after cooling down.
- Optional: cut into squares or not.

By J. Martinez

Sheet Cake Fruit Cookies

Who would of thought to combine nectarines and cookies? With this recipe you can combine your two favorite treats together, and add a dollop of vanilla ice cream to top off this dessert..

Total Time: 40 minutes
Makes: 20 Servings

INGREDIENTS:
- 1 cup butter, softened
- 1 cup sugar
- 4 eggs
- 2 cups flour
- ½ tsp. salt
- 6 nectarines

Topping:
- 2/3 cup sugar
- 2 tbsp. cinnamon

DIRECTIONS:
- Set the oven to 375 degrees
- Combine the sugar and shortening together to create the cream.
- Next, add the eggs and stir with enthusiasm.
- Add the dry ingredients in a separate bowl. Slowly add the cream mixture to the dry mixture
- On the Copper Crisper cookie sheet, spread the batter.
- Slice the nectarines thick and place the fruit closely together.
- Brush the cinnamon and sugar together on top of the fruit.
- Bake for 40 minutes.
- Remove, cool and enjoy with some vanilla ice cream.

Caramel Candy Pecan Pie Cookies

This is a great recipe to make any time of the year. But, if you want to wait for Christmas, don't forget to leave a couple out for Santa.

Total Time: 90 minutes
Makes: 14 Servings

INGREDIENTS:

Dough:
- 1 cup unsalted butter
- 4 oz. cream cheese
- ¾ cups brown sugar
- ¾ cups sugar
- 1 tbsp. vanilla
- ¼ tsp. salt
- ½ cups pecans, finely chopped
- 2 ½ cups all-purpose flour

Filling:
- ¼ cup unsalted butter, melted
- ¼ cup sugar
- ¼ cup corn syrup
- 1 egg yolk
- 2 tsp. bourbon
- 1 pinch of coarse salt
- 1 cup pecans, finely chopped
-
- Caramel drizzle:
- 4 oz. caramel candies, unwrapped
- 2 tbsp. heavy cream

DIRECTIONS:
- Set the oven to 350 degrees.
- Start, by mixing the cream cheese and the butter in an electric mixer on medium heat until well blended.
- Add in the sugars and mix for 3 minutes, and then mix in the vanilla.
- Moving to low speed, add in the pecans, salt and flour until mixed well.
- Cover and refrigerate for 60 minutes.
- Next, in another bowl mix the melted butter, corn syrup, egg yolk, sugar, vanilla and salt together.
- Mix until blended well and then add in the pecans.
- Take the dough out of the fridge, and roll pieces into balls.
- Place each ball on the Copper Crisper cookie sheet 2 inches apart from each other.
- Make a round indention in each piece of dough with your thumb.
- Pour some of the filling mixture into each indentation.
- Cook for 18 minutes and let cool when done.
- Lastly, mix the heavy cream and candies in a microwaveable bowl.
- Heat for 20 seconds at a time, stirring until the mixture is smooth.
- Drizzle over the cookies.
- Serve and enjoy.

Honey Plum Tarts

Fruit and honey is an age old snack. Combine it with crust and bake it and you have a golden dessert that will melt in your mouth.

Total Time: 30 minutes
Makes: 6 Servings

INGREDIENTS:
- 1 14 oz. package puff pastry, thawed
- 1 lb. red plums, wedged
- ¼ cup sugar
- 1 tbsp. honey
- Sea salt to taste
- Ground pepper to taste

DIRECTIONS:
- Set the oven to 425 degrees.
- Start by cutting the pastry into six 4 inch squares and place on the Copper Crisper cookie sheet.
- Take a fork and make holes all over the pastry.
- Place the plums on top of the pastry, but make sure to leave half an inch all the way around the pastry.
- Sprinkle the pepper, and sugar on top of the plums.
- Bake the tarts for 30 minutes, rotate halfway through.
- Lightly sprinkle the honey and salt a few minutes before it is done baking.
- Remove, serve and enjoy.

By J. Martinez

Fruity Infused Pizza

This is a treat for the whole family. Pizza with fruit, who wouldn't want to try this? It is one of our favorites that even celebrities love!

Total Time: 30 minutes
Makes: 20 Servings

INGREDIENTS:
- 2 packages sugar cookie dough
- 8 oz. cream cheese, strawberry whipped
- 1 lime
- 1 lemon
- Strawberries to taste
- Blueberries taste
- Blackberries to taste
- Bananas to taste
- Kiwi to taste
- Oranges to taste
- Peaches to taste

DIRECTIONS:
- Set the oven at 350 degrees.
- Spread the cookie dough onto the Copper Crisper cookie sheet and roll flat.
- Bake for 30 minutes and let cool.
- While cooking, mix the cream cheese, and lime juice together.
- Spread the cream cheese mixture on the cookie crust.
- Layer the sliced fruit in rows on top of the cream cheese.
- Serve and enjoy.

Cinnamon Style Donuts

Homemade donuts – a special treat the kids will love to eat. They will beg to help you in the kitchen.

Total Time: 8 minutes
Makes: 4 Servings

INGREDIENTS:
Doughnuts:
- 2 tbsp. butter, at room temperature
- ½ cup sugar
- 2 ¼ cup plain flour
- 1 ½ tsp. baking powder
- 1 tsp. salt
- 2 large egg yolks
- ½ cup sour cream
- ¼ cup butter, melted

Cinnamon sugar
- 1/3 cup caster sugar
- 1 tsp. cinnamon

DIRECTIONS:
- Set the oven temperature to 350 degrees.
- Mix the butter and sugar together in a bowl.
- Add the egg yolks and stir well.
- In another bowl separate the flour, baking powder and salt. Slowly stir in 1/3 of the flour and half of the sour cream.
- When mixed add in the rest and place in the fridge.
- Pull out a cutting board and add some flour.
- Roll out the dough in doughnut shapes.
- Rub butter on all sides of the dough and drop in the Crisper Tray .
- Cook for 8 minutes.
- When done, run more butter and roll in the cinnamon sugar.
- Serve and enjoy.

By J. Martinez

Oven Cinnamon French Toast Sticks

A healthier option for a famous breakfast dish – with less work than cooking the traditional way.

Total Time: 8 minutes
Makes: 4 Servings

INGREDIENTS:
- *4 pieces of sliced bread, whatever kind and thickness desired*
- *2 tbsp. butter*
- *2 eggs, gently beaten*
- *1 tsp. salt*
- *1 tsp. cinnamon*
- *1 tsp. nutmeg*
- *1 tsp. ground cloves*
- *Icing sugar and maple sugar for garnish and serving*

DIRECTIONS:
- Set the oven temperature to 350 degrees.
- Beat two eggs together in a medium bowl.
- Slowly add salt, cinnamon, nutmeg, and ground cloves.
- Smear butter on both sides of the bread and make into strips.
- Place in the egg mixture and then in the Crisper Tray .
- Cook for 2 minutes and remove from the oven.
- Coat each of the strips with cooking spray and cook for 6 more minutes.
- Serve when golden brown.
- Add icing sugar, whip cream and maple sugar for taste.

Oven Fried Bananas

Try this lightly fried and healthy snack with a taste of cinnamon and sugar. It is a hit the family will be dying to eat over and over again.

Total Time: 14 minutes
Makes: 4 Servings

INGREDIENTS:
- *3 tbsp. vegan butter substitute*
- *8 ripe bananas*
- *2 whole eggs*
- *½ cup flour*
- *1 cup breadcrumbs*

DIRECTIONS:
- Set the oven temperature to 350 degrees.
- Turn the stove onto medium and heat the butter substitute.
- Add the breadcrumbs to the heated butter in the pan, and stir for 4 minutes.
- Pour into a medium size bowl and set aside.
- Peel the bananas and cut them in half.
- Take each half and roll in the corn flour, eggs, and then breadcrumbs.
- Place inside the Crisper Tray .
- Lightly pour the cinnamon sugar on each banana.
- Bake for 10 minutes.
- Serve when cool and enjoy.

By J. Martinez

Pastry Wrapped Milky Ways

The children will love this type of fried candy without all of the grease. Pastry wrapped milky ways will taste like a treat from the fair, without the stomachache.

Total Time: 25 minutes
Makes: 4 Servings

INGREDIENTS:
- *1 package puff pastry*
- *1 bag mini milky ways*

DIRECTIONS:
- Make sure to cut the puff pastry into square shapes.
- Wrap each individual square around one mini milky way.
- Seal all of the edges.
- Preheat the oven to the temperature on the pastry package.
- Place all wrapped candy bars in the Crisper Tray
- Bake according to the package.
- Cool when done.
- Serve and enjoy.

GLUTEN FREE:

For Those With Special Eating Needs

This is a section for those who have special eating needs and yes we understand that! We have put together some of the most flavorful foods for you in this menu area. Eating healthy is in, and keeping your body as healthy as you can is what these foods are for. Bake it...eat it...enjoy it...LOVE IT! ;)

By J. Martinez

Gluten Free Monsterlicious Cookie Bars

Perfect treat for Halloween parties! Use black and orange M&Ms just for fun.

Total Time: 20 minutes
Makes: 20 Servings

INGREDIENTS:
- *6 cup brown sugar*
- *1 cup sugar*
- *1 stick butter, salted*
- *2 cups peanut butter, creamy*
- *3 eggs*
- *1 tbsp. vanilla*
- *1 ½ cups quick oats*
- *3 cups old fashioned oats*
- *1 tsp. baking soda*
- *2 cups M&Ms*
- *1 cup chocolate chips*

DIRECTIONS:
- Set oven to 350 degrees.
- Mix the peanut butter, butter, brown sugar and sugar together in a large bowl.
- Next, blend the eggs and the vanilla together with the dry ingredients. Then the oats, baking soda and M&Ms and mix with a spatula until mixed well.
- Spread out on the Copper Crisper cookie sheet, and sprinkle more M&Ms on top if desired. Just make sure to press into the dough
- Bake for 20 minutes.
- Cool for an hour.
- Serve and enjoy

Gluten Free Pork Pan Nachos

Summer is a perfect time for Barbequing. But, have you ever thought of combining pulled pork and nachos together? Well, you are in for a treat because this dish will be the talk of the neighborhood.

Total Time: 10 minutes
Makes: 20 Servings

INGREDIENTS:
- 1 bag corn tortilla chips
- 2 cups pulled pork, cooked
- 8 oz. of sharp cheddar
- 8 oz. Monterey jack
- ½ cup black beans
- 2 tomatoes, diced
- Pickled jalapenos to taste
- Cilantro to taste

DIRECTIONS:
- Set the oven to 350 degrees.
- Spread out the corn chips on the Copper Crisper cookie sheet and sprinkle the cheese on top.
- Cook for 6 minutes.
- Add the meat on top and cook for an additional 3 minutes.
- Remove and top with the remaining ingredients.
- Serve and enjoy.

By J. Martinez

Gluten Free Oven Crispy Green Beans

Fried everything seems to be the motto these days, but it can really put on the pounds. Well, don't worry. With this gluten free, no oil fry recipe, you can rest easy about packing on the pounds..

Total Time: 30 minutes
Makes: 4 Servings

INGREDIENTS:
- 2 dozen green beans, cut and drained

Batter:
- 1 cup Pamela's gluten free pizza mix
- ½ tsp. salt
- 2 tsp. sugar
- ½ tsp. black pepper
- ¼ cayenne pepper
- 1 tbsp. butter, melted
- 1 egg yolk
- 2 egg whites, whipped
- 1.2 cup gluten free beer

DIRECTIONS:
- Set the oven to 425 degrees.
- Whisk the salt, flour, sugar, pepper and cayenne in a large bowl.
- Beat the eggs, butter, wine and beer together in a separate bowl, and then add with the dry ingredients.
- Pat the green beans dry before adding them into the mix. Coat thoroughly.
- Place the green beans on the Copper Crisper cookie sheet and bake for 15 minutes until crispy.
- Remove, serve and enjoy.

Gluten Free Chicken and Vegetables

This is a wonderful comfort food dish the family will love. Something you can whip out during rainy days, to bring the family closer together.

Total Time: 45 minutes
Makes: 4 Servings

INGREDIENTS:
- 1 bell pepper, red
- 1 onion, sliced
- 1 zucchini, sliced
- 1 yellow squash, sliced;2
- 2 ¾ cups gluten free all-purpose baking flour
- 1 tbsp. baking powder
- 2 tsps. Salt
- 1 cup gluten free beer
- ½ cup sparkling water
- 4 skinless, boneless chicken breast halves

DIRECTIONS:
- Start out whisking the salt, baking powder and flour together in a large bowl.
- Next, add the beer and sparkling water. Combine thoroughly.
- Set the oven to 350 degrees
- Place the Copper Crisper Tray on top of the cookie sheet.
- Whisk flour, baking powder, and salt together in a large bowl; add beer and sparkling water. Stir until batter just combined.
- Dip the bell pepper, onion, and zucchini into the batter. Get rid of the excess and bake in the oven for 15 minutes.
- Remove from the oven and set aside.
- Dip the chicken breasts into the rest of the batter and set inside the Crisper Tray . Cook for 30 minutes. Remove; serve with sauce of your choice.

By J. Martinez

Gluten Free Sizzling Crispy Fried Fish

You can make this sizzling southern dish without compromising all of the taste.
Total Time: 45 minutes
Makes: 4 Servings

INGREDIENTS:
- *¾ gluten free Bisquick*
- *¾ cup gluten free beer*
- *1 tbsp. Old Bay Seasoning*
- *½ tsp. garlic powder*
- *4 fish fillets cut in half*
- *¼ gluten free Bisquick, for dusting fish*
- *Onion salt to taste*

DIRECTIONS:
- Set the oven to 250 degrees
- Wash the fish and pat dry.
- Cut each piece in half.
- Dust with the Bisquick.
- Mix the fish together with the Bisquick, beer, seasoning, and garlic powder together in a bowl.
- Set each piece in the Copper Crisper Tray and cook for 30 minutes until golden brown.
- Remove, serve and enjoy.

Gluten Free Savory Southern Fried Chicken

This is the best fried chicken recipe that you will ever eat. You might even forget that its gluten free and downright healthier for you.
Total Time: 120 minutes
Makes: 8 Servings

INGREDIENTS:
- 5 lbs. chicken legs, quartered
- 1 tsp. salt
- 1 tsp. pepper
- 1 tsp. garlic powder
- 1 tsp. paprika
- 1 cup coconut flour

DIRECTIONS:
- Set the oven to 350 degrees.
- Mix the chicken, salt, pepper, garlic powder and paprika together in a large bowl or container.
- Massage the spices and refrigerate for at least two hours.
- Remove from the freezer and dip the chicken in the coconut flour
- Place the pieces in the Copper Crisper Tray and bake for 30 minutes or until the chicken is cooked all the way through.
- Serve with mashed potatoes, or potato salad.

By J. Martinez

Gluten Free Oven Baked Buttermilk Doughnuts

Homemade donuts without all the oil and grease. This will soon become one of your favorite treats.

Total Time: 40 minutes
Makes: 12 Servings

INGREDIENTS:
- 1 egg
- 1 cup buttermilk
- 2 tbsp. butter, melted
- 2 ½ cups Betty Crocker All Purpose Gluten Free Rice Flour Blend
- ½ cup sugar
- ¼ tsp. ground cinnamon
- ¼ tsp. ground nutmeg
- 1 tsp. baking soda
- 1 tsp. salt
- 1 tsp. xanthan gum
- ½ tsp. gluten free baking powder

Chocolate glaze:
- ½ cup powdered sugar
- 1 tsp. unsweetened baking cocoa
- 1 tbsp. butter, melted
- 4 tsp. milk

DIRECTIONS:
- Set the oven to 350 degrees
- In a large bowl beat the egg, buttermilk and 2 tbsp. melted butter until blended thoroughly.
- In another bowl, mix the rest of the dough ingredients, and slowly fold into dry egg mixture.
- Sprinkle hands on the dough while mixing if necessary. Cover and let rest for 15 minutes.
- In a separate bowl nix the chocolate glaze ingredients. Remember to stir enough milk for your desired smoothed consistency. Set aside.

- On a work surface: sprinkle flour and roll out the dough. Using a cookie cutter, cut in 3 inch rounds.
- Place the doughnuts and holes in the Copper Crisper Tray and cook for 8 minutes.
- Dip each in the glaze and serve warm.

By J. Martinez

Gluten Free Parmesan Style Pork Chops

Parmesan baked on top of your pork chop gives a cheesy flavor that will dance in your mouth and make you reach for more.

Total Time: 20 minutes
Makes: 4 Servings

INGREDIENTS:
- 4 boneless pork chops
- ½ cup rice crumbs
- ¾ parmesan cheese, shredded and grated
- 1 egg
- ¼ cup gluten free flour
- ¼ tsp. garlic powder
- ¼ tsp. Italian seasoning
- ¼ tsp. parsley
- Salt and pepper to taste
- Season salt to taste

DIRECTIONS:
- Set the oven to 40 0degrees.
- In a small bowl, pour the flour, salt and pepper together.
- In a separate bowl, pour the parmesan, bread crumbs, season salts parsley and garlic powder together.
- Place the egg in a separate bowl.
- Dip the pork chops in the flour mixture, then egg and lastly the parmesan.
- Place in the Copper Crisper Tray and cook for 15 minutes.
- Serve with mashed potatoes or rice.\

Gluten Free Brown Sugar Oven Fried Steak

This brown sugar oven fried steak will excite your taste buds. Cooked with the vegetables and served with rice, you will have an amazing meal.

Total Time: 60 minutes
Makes: 4 Servings

INGREDIENTS:
- 2 carrots, finely shredded
- 2 scallions, shredded
- 2 zucchinis, shredded
- 2 yellow squash, shredded
- 1 garlic clove, finely chopped
- 14 oz. sirloin steak, trimmed
- 2 eggs, beaten
- ½ tsp. salt
- 4 tbsp. cornstarch

Sauce:
- 4 tbsp. brown sugar
- 3 tbsp. balsamic vinegar
- 2 tbsp. soy sauce

DIRECTIONS:
- Set the oven to 350 degrees
- Cut the beef into thin slices and set aside. Then shred all of the vegetables.
- Mix the eggs, salt and cornstarch together with a fork.
- Dip the beef in the batter and set aside.
- Pour all the sauce ingredients in a measuring cup and set aside.
- Place the beef in the center of the Copper Crisper cookie sheet and add all of the vegetables around it so they are spread out evenly.
- Cook for 15 minutes. Remove and serve with rice.\

By J. Martinez

Gluten Free Garlic Cilantro Chicken

Is your mouth watering yet...well ours is! All I can say about this chicken dish is... You can never have enough garlic! Feel free to add more and smile the entire time you are enjoying this succulent dish!

Total Time: 30 min
Makes: 4-6 Servings

INGREDIENTS:
- *2lbs boneless skinless chicken breasts (6 small breasts)*
- *1 tbsp. olive or avocado oil*
- *1 tsp kosher salt*
- *1 tsp freshly-ground black pepper*
- *1 tsp garlic powder*
- *1 tsp paprika*
- *half a handful of finely chopped cilantro*

DIRECTIONS:
Marinade for this chicken dish:
- In a large container (preferably a bowl) fill with 2 quarts of water that is warm. Add 4 tbsp. of kosher salt and 2 tbsp. of garlic powder.
- Add the chicken breasts and mix around until all of the chicken has absorbed the salt mixture, soaking for about 10-12 minutes.

Note: A second option is to refrigerate in covered container between 4-5 hours.

Cooking instructions:
- Pre heat oven to 350 degrees.
- Take the chicken from your marinade and pat dry.
- Lightly brush the chicken with the oil mixture.
- Sprinkle the chicken with fresh ground pepper and paprika.
- Place each filet of chicken in your Crisper Tray so it is flat.
- It is OK if they touch but try not to pack them in too tight.
- Bake Chicken for approximately 10-12 min.
- Pull out the Crisper Tray and sprinkle the Cilantro atop the chicken evenly.
- Bake for another 7-10 minutes.
- Check the chicken browning and crispness on the outside, it should be done.

Gluten Free Garlic Jalapeno Shrimp

Wow! This dish is one of our favorite and when you make this one, you will see why! If you like seafood then you will become a "Jalapeno Shrimp Lover!"

Total Time: 30 min
Makes: 4-6 Serving

INGREDIENTS

- *1 to 2 pounds medium sized shrimp*
- *1 cup Gluten Free Bread Crumbs*
- *2 tsp. sea salt*
- *1 tbsp. garlic powder*
- *1 jalapeno pepper (use 2 jalapenos for more kick)*
- *¼ tsp. pepper*
- *1 egg, lightly beaten*
- *2 tbsp. water*
- *1 1emon*

DIRECTIONS

- Pre heat oven to 350 degrees.
- In a large zip lock bag, add the bread crumbs, garlic, rosemary, sea salt and pepper; shake the mixture to combine all of the ingredients.
- Combine the eggs and water, In a small bowl like container.
- Take each piece of fish and lightly dip the pieces in egg mixture.
- Individually shake the bag of shrimp one piece at a time in the bag to coat.
- Place each piece of fish in your Crisper Tray .
- Bake in the oven until you see the shrimp turn a nice golden brown and crispy!
- Before serving…cut the lemon in half and squeeze the lemon over each piece of fish for extra flavor.

By J. Martinez

Gluten-Free Bacon Stuffed Twice-Baked cheesy Garlic Potatoes

Total Time: 1hr
Serving: 6-8 (6 potatoes cut in half will make 12 filling halves)

INGREDIENTS
- *6 Potatoes (scrubbed and washed)*
- *2 cups shredded cheddar cheese*
- *1 cup bacon (real bacon)*
- *1/4 cup garlic*
- *1/4 fresh sweet onion*
- *1 cup sour cream*
- *1/4 cup butter*
- *1 tsp parsley*
- *Pinch of Sea salt and pepper to taste*

DIRECTIONS
- Preheat oven to 425 degrees.
- Take a fork to poke some holes all over the potatoes so they breath when baking.
- Coat potatoes with olive oil (avocado oil)
- Wrap each potato with foil and put them on your crisper evenly on the center oven rack for 50 minutes.
- Remember to put the cookie sheet under.
- Test potatoes by seeing if they are softly firm. If so, take out of the oven.
- Slice potatoes in half longways and stake a spoon to scoop out filling.
- Mix the filling with butter, 1-1/4 cup cheese, 3/4 cup bacon, garlic, onion and parsley and add sour cream. You may want to add in the sea salt and pepper at this point.
- Start filling your potato skins with the ingredients that you just mixed.
- Before putting back in the oven, add the remainder of bacon and cheese.
- Place back on the crisper with cookies sheet under
- Bake for another 12-15 minutes.
- You can serve with sour cream. Salsa is one of our favorites...your preference from here. Yum!

Gluten Free Spicy Crusted Asparagus

This is a dish that will go great with any entrée and make your mouth water! Get daily dose of vitamins and minerals when indulging in this amazing crispy dish!

Total Time: 30 min
Makes: 4-6 Serving

INGREDIENTS
- *1 pounds medium to large stalked fresh Asparagus*
- *1 cup Gluten Free Bread Crumbs*
- *2 tsp. sea salt*
- *1 tbsp. garlic powder*
- *1 cayenne pepper (or use 1 tbsp. of cayenne powder*
- *¼ tsp. pepper*
- *1 egg, lightly beaten*
- *2 tbsp. water*
- *1 pack of goad cheese (to sprinkle atop)*

DIRECTIONS
- Pre heat oven to 350 degrees.
- In a large zip lock bag, add the bread crumbs, garlic, cayenne pepper, sea salt and pepper; shake the mixture to combine all of the ingredients.
- Combine the eggs and water, In a small bowl like container.
- Take the asparagus and lightly dip the pieces in egg mixture.
- Put the Asparagus in the bag and shake till it is all coated nicely.
- Place the asparagus in your Crisper Tray . (try to space out evenly)
- Bake in the oven till the asparagus turns golden crispy brown about 15 minutes!
- While serving, add the goat cheese on top of the asparagus.
- Makes a great side dish!

By J. Martinez

Gluten-Free Garlic Mint Mozzarella Stuffed Meatballs

All we have to say about these meatballs is…"YUM!" We are going into another level of cooking when we crafted this one up for you. This is something that you will enjoy for years to come! :)

Total Time: 30 min
Makes: 4 Serving

INGREDIENTS
- 1 1/2 pounds ground beef
- 1 egg beaten
- 1/4 cup gluten-free Italian-style bread crumbs*
- 2 tablespoons of minced garlic
- mozzarella cheese sticks cut into square cubed sections
- 2 tbsp. avocado oil (can also use coconut oil)
- 1/2 handful of fresh mint leaves finely chopped

DIRECTIONS
- Pre heat oven to 425.
- Mix the ground beef, egg and bread crumbs together thoroughly in a mixing bowl till the egg mixes through.
- Add the garlic and chopped up mint leaves and finish mixing thoroughly.
- Shape the meatballs into 15-20 medium sized rounded balls
- In the middle of your meatballs, slide one mozzarella cube & seal the meatball around the cheese evenly so the cheese does not run out while baking.
- Place all meatballs in the crisper and space evenly.
- Lightly brush the meatballs with the avocado oil (or coconut oil)
- Cook for approximately 20-25 min or until the meatballs brown nicely. (If some of the cheese starts to drip, don't worry. The Crisper cookie sheet that is under the tray will catch it so there is no mess).
- Best served with spaghetti and pasta sauce to make a fantastic meal addition!

Gluten Free Crispy Lemon Dill Fish filet

Get that fancy restaurant flavor right at home when making this dish. Not only is it nice and crispy, but it's sinfully nothing less than deliciousness! Enjoy!

Total Time: 30 min
Makes: 4-6 Serving

INGREDIENTS
- 1 to 2 pounds fish (tilapia, halibut or salmon)
- 1 cup Gluten Free Bread Crumbs
- 2 tsp. sea salt
- 1 tbsp. garlic powder
- t tsp. dill weed powder
- 1/4 tsp. pepper
- 1 egg, lightly beaten
- 2 tbsp. water
- 1 1emon

DIRECTIONS
- Pre heat oven to 350 degrees.
- In a large zip lock bag, add the bread crumbs, garlic, dill weed powder, sea salt and pepper; shake the mixture to combine all of the ingredients.
- Combine the eggs and water, In a small bowl like container.
- Take each piece of fish and lightly dip the pieces in egg mixture.
- Individually shake the bag of fish one piece at a time in the zip bag to coat.
- Place each piece of fish in your Crisper Tray .
- Bake in the oven until you see the fish turn a nice golden brown and crispy!
- Before serving…cut the lemon in half and squeeze the lemon over each piece of fish for extra flavor.
- Delicious!

By J. Martinez

Gluten Free Almond Crusted Garlic Basil Chicken Strips

Everyone will love you for making this dish and is a very healthy way to fall in love with chicken strips!

Total Time: 20 minutes
Makes: 4 Servings

INGREDIENTS
- 4 medium boneless skinless chicken breasts (cut into tender strips)
- 1 cup almonds
- 2 small eggs (lightly beaten)
- 1 tbsp. olive oil (avocado oil can substitute)
- 1/4 cup Gluten Free all-purpose flour
- 1 tbsp. garlic powder
- 1 tsp minced garlic
- 1 tsp black pepper
- 1 tsp cinnamon
- 1 tsp paprika
- 1 tbsp. basil
- 1 Jalapeno pepper

DIRECTIONS
- Preheat your oven to 400 degrees.
- The eggs, flour and almonds will all mix separately. Will need three bowls.
- Beat the eggs lightly (for dipping the chicken) and move to the side for later.
- Put the almonds in a food processor and blend them up very fine.
- Add in the garlic powder, minced garlic, black pepper, paprika, basil and cinnamon into the ground almonds and mix together.
- In the flour, one at a time, dip the chicken strips allowing to coat all over.
- Use the egg bowl and dip each of the strips and drip the extra egg off.
- Last you will place the chicken in the finely ground almond mixture to coat the chicken. Make sure you press the chicken into the almond mixture with your fingers to ensure they are coated nicely.
- Place each of the strips of chicken into your crisper with the baking sheet underneath.

- Cook for about 10-12 minutes.
- Open oven and lightly brush the chicken tops with oil and bake for another 5-6 minutes or until the tenders turn golden brown in color and check to make sure chicken is cooked entirely. (atop with diced jalapenos - optional)

By J. Martinez

Gluten Free Cinnamon Date Cranberry Oatmeal Cookies

Everyone loves cookies, but these cookies will make everyone fall in love with you! Just like grandma used to make but now in a more healthy way! Enjoy!

Total Time: 25 minutes
Makes: 20-25 Cookies

INGREDIENTS
- 1 1/2 cups gluten free rolled oats
- 1 cup gluten free oat flour
- 2 flax eggs (I used flax egg replacements)
- 1/2 cup maple syrup
- 2 tsp cinnamon
- 1 tsp vanilla extract
- 1 tsp baking powder
- 1 tsp baking soda
- 1/4 cup unsweetened applesauce
- 1/4 cup dates
- 1/4 cup cranberries (crushed)
- 1/2 tsp sea salt

DIRECTIONS
- Preheat oven to 350 degrees.
- Take all of your ingredients and combine in one bowl and mix together.
- Mix in the dates and cranberries together and evenly.
- Place the cookies onto your crisper baking sheet baking sheet. (Note: for more crispy cookies place the cookies onto the Crisper Tray with the cookie sheet underneath.)
- Bake for 10-12 minutes. The cookies will be hot so let them cool for about 15 minutes before taking them out.

MARINADES:

Hand Selected For Meats & Veggies:

Marinating your vegetables...You Betcha!!! The whole idea is to get the most flavor out of your food to get the best results for your cooking! There are so many people who do not know some of the tips and tricks that the "Professional Cooks" in all of your favorite restaurants know! That's why you keep running out to spend endless amounts of money to get some of these flavors that you love. Well those days are over! We have packed this section with our 10 BEST MARINADES that we know you will love. Some of these marinades that you see in this section will give your food that most amazing flavors and you will grow to love your foods even more after using some of these tasty flavors on your foods...Just try us! Absolutely the most delicious meat soaking juices that money can buy! Enjoy these succulent flavors of what we have put together for you and your foods that you want to indulge! Enjoy ;)

By J. Martinez

Horseradish Apple Cider Garlic Marinade:

INGREDIENTS:
- 1 egg
- 1 cup mayonnaise
- 1/2 cup apple cider vinegar
- 4 tbsp. of garlic juice
- 2 tbsp. of horseradish sauce
- 1/3 cup sugar
- 1/2 cup dry mustard

DIRECTIONS:
- Combine all of these ingredients, except the garlic and mayonnaise, in a blender for best results!
- Prepare and warm up these ingredients in a pan on medium heat.
- You will start to see the sauce get thicker.
- After it thickens from the heat mix in 4 tbsp. Of garlic juice 1 cup mayonnaise and stir the mixture!

Garlic Rosemary Cinnamon Honey Marinade

INGREDIENTS:
- 2 tbsp. Honey
- 1/2 tsp. Cinnamon
- 1 tsp. Rosemary
- 2 tsp. Chopped fresh parsley
- 1/2 cup onion (minced)
- 1/4 cup fresh lemon juice
- 1/4 cup avocado oil
- 2 tbsp. Low sodium soy sauce
- 2 cloves garlic (crushed or minced)
- 1 tbsp. Ginger (grated fresh)

DIRECTIONS:
- Combine all of these ingredients together in a blender for best results!

By J. Martinez

White Wine Cayenne Pepper Kick Marinade

INSTRUCTIONS:
- 2 1/2 cups white wine (dry)
- 1/2 teaspoon cayenne pepper
- 1/2 teaspoon garlic powder
- 1 teaspoon onion powder
- 1/2 tsp. Parsley
- 1/2 tsp. Fresh ground pepper
- 1 jalapeno pepper (minced)
- 1/2 cup soy sauce

DIRECTIONS:
- Combine all of these ingredients together in a blender for best results!

Red Wine Sweet Cajun Texas Tabasco Marinade

INSTRUCTIONS:
- 1/3 cup soy sauce & 1/2 cup red wine
- 2 tablespoons Cajun seasoning
- 2 tablespoons Tabasco seasoning
- 2 tablespoons minced garlic
- 2 tablespoons brown sugar
- 1/2 teaspoon cinnamon
- 1 tablespoon tomato paste
- 1 teaspoon freshly ground black pepper
- 1 splash of lemon juice

DIRECTIONS:
- Combine all of these ingredients together in a blender for best results!

By J. Martinez

Dill Lemon Pepper Basil Marinade

INGREDIENTS:
- *2/3 cup lemon juice*
- *2 cloves garlic (minced)*
- *1 teaspoon pepper (fresh ground)*
- *1/2 teaspoon basil*
- *1/2 teaspoon dill.*
- *3 oz. water*
- *2 teaspoons chicken bouillon (granules)*

DIRECTIONS:
- Combine all of these ingredients together in a blender for best results!

Louisiana Liquid Smoke Flavored Marinade

INGREDIENTS:
- 1/4 cup lime juice
- 1/4 cup avocado oil
- 1/3 cup water
- 1 tablespoon vinegar
- 2 teaspoons soy sauce (low sodium)
- 2 teaspoons Worcestershire sauce
- 2-3 drops of liquid smoke
- 1 clove garlic, minced
- 1/2 teaspoon chili powder
- 1/2 teaspoon beef bouillon paste
- 1/2 teaspoon ground cumin
- 1/2 teaspoon dried oregano
- 1/4 teaspoon ground black pepper

DIRECTIONS:
- Combine all of these ingredients together in a blender for best results!

By J. Martinez

Pineapple Raspberry Flavor Twister Marinade

INGREDIENTS:
- 1/2 cup raspberry preserves
- 1/2 teaspoon lemon juice
- 2 tablespoons rice vinegar
- 1/2 teaspoon minced garlic
- 1/2 teaspoon dried basil
- 1/2 cup pineapple juice
- 1/2 cup soy sauce

DIRECTIONS:
- Combine all of these ingredients together in a blender for best results!

Garlic Italian Marinating Magnifier

INGREDIENTS:
- 1/2 cup Italian dressing
- 1/2 teaspoon lemon juice
- 1 tablespoon minced garlic
- 1/2 teaspoon dried basil
- 1/2 teaspoon Tabasco sauce

DIRECTIONS:
- Combine all of these ingredients together in a blender for best results!

By J. Martinez

Mild Marinade Seafood Soaker

INSTRUCTIONS:
- *1/2 cup onion (minced)*
- *1/4 cup fresh lemon juice*
- *1/8 cup avocado oil*
- *1/8 cup butter (almond butter best)*
- *2 tsp. Chopped fresh parsley*
- *Sprinkle of sea salt*
- *Sprinkle of fresh ground pepper to taste*

DIRECTIONS:
- Combine all of these ingredients together in a blender for best results!

White Wine Hot Peppered Garlic Marinade

INSTRUCTIONS:
- *2 1/2 cups white wine (dry)*
  - 1/8 cup avocado oil
  - 1 tbsp. Old bay seasoning
  - 1/4 cup fresh lemon juice
  - 2 tsp. Chopped parsley (fresh)
  - 2 tsp. Paprika
  - 2 tsp. Fresh ground pepper
  - 1 tsp. crushed red pepper

DIRECTIONS:
- Combine all of these ingredients together in a blender for best results!

By J. Martinez

NEXT ON THE LIST!

Here's What You Do Now…

If you were please with our book then **please leave us a review on amazon where you purchased this book!** In the world of an author who writes books independently, your reviews are not only touching but important so that we know you like the material we have prepared for "you" our audience! So leave us a review…we would love to see that you enjoyed our book!

If for any reason that you were less than happy with your experience then send me an email at **Feedback@HealthyLifestyleRecipes.org** and let me know how we can better your experience. We always come out with a few volumes of our books and will possibly be able to address some of your concerns. Do keep in mind that we strive to do our best to give you the highest quality of what "we the independent authors" pour our heart, soul and tears into.

I am very happy to create new and exciting recipes and do appreciate your purchase. I thank you for your many great reviews and comments! With a warm heart! ~ J. Martinez "Professional Loving Chef" …Xoxo ;)

ABOUT THE AUTHOR

J. Martinez is a Self Trained Professional Gourmet Chef that has over 15 years experience with her craft. These special recipes within this book are some of her own personal favorites that have been in the homes of many famous celebrities. Her profession calls for her to visit many well known names to cater special events and cook up some of the best meals she can offer. In her spare time she loves taking walks on the beach, reading and of course stirring up new creations to make in the kitchen for everyone to enjoy!

By J. Martinez

FREE BOOKS!!

New Books Pro Cooking Tips, & Recipes Sent to Your Email

For our current readers...if you like receiving free books, pro cooking tips & recipes to add to your collection, then **this is for you!** This is for promoting our material to our current members so you can **review our new books on Amazon** and give us feed back when we launch new books we are publishing! This helps us determine how we can make our books better for you, our audience! Just go to the url below and leave your name and email. We will send you a complimentary book about once a month.

Get My Free Book

http://www.Healthylifestylerecipes.org/Freebook2review

OTHER RECOMMEND BOOKS!

1: If you are looking for amazing foods that go great for any occasion then you should check out "Ceramic Titanium Cookbook by Sasha Hassler & Allison August! There are many delicious foods and desserts that can be made in this non-stick ceramic titanium fry pan. With over 99 different recipes you will become a large fan of this great Amazon selling cookbook! Click the link below: http://www.amazon.com/Ceramic-Titanium-Cookbook-Delicious-Nutritious/dp/1545047995

2: A second must have book that we highly recommend is our Cuisinart 3-in-1 Burger Press Cookbook! **"Monster Burger Recipes!"** This book is packed with some amazing ways to "burger your burgers!" Over 99 reasons to be the life of the party and control those bragging rights. After you try some of these "mile high" burgers you will never go back to the old way it was done in the past! So check this book out for yourself and grab one for your friends! It makes a great gift and even a better surprise!: link below!
http://www.Amazon.Com/Cuisinart-Burger-Press-Cookbook-Entertainment/Dp/1539557685

3: A Third Classic Book That We Highly Recommend Is **Our Presto Electric Skillet Cookbook!** You Can Do The **"Electric Slide"** With These Recipes Because They Are Nonstick And Slide Around In The Pan! This Book Will Show You How To Cut That Electric Bill In Half By Turning On That Electric Skillet And Whipping Up Some Of Those Savory Delicious Meals That Are Featured In This Easy To Make Recipe Book. **We've Got You Covered On All Types Of Meals You Can Make With This Skillet.** This Recipe Book Will Show You How To: Stir Fry, Sauté, Bake, Warm And Even Whip Up Some Of The Most Delicious Desserts, "Just Like Grandma Used To Make!" Just Check It Out!
http://www.Amazon.Com/Our-Presto-Electric-Skillet-Cookbook-Ebook/Dp/B01N46QL1T

4: Our last recommendation is **Our KitchenAid Ice Cream Recipe Book.** "tickle your taste buds!" With these impulsive, flavored recipes to get that alternative dessert deliciousness! We show you how to get the most out of your kitchen aid ice cream maker by **stuffing this book with the most impressive ice cream, sorbet, frozen yogurt, gelato and milkshake's that are very easy to make, simple & sweet, yummy & tasty, but "sinfully delicious & creative!"** For your friends, family...or that special someone...w can make incredibly healthy desserts! This amazing book even has a one-of-a-kind exclusive adult section for those who dare to spike desserts creatively! ;)
http://www.Amazon.Com/Kitchenaid-Cream-Maker-Recipe-Book/Dp/154283614X

RECIPE NOTES:

RECIPE NOTES: